ANGKOR WAT

TOM VATER

Contents

ANGKOR WAT

SIEM REAP AND ANGKOR

The magnificent temple ruins of Angkor are amongst the great, ancient wonders of the world. The gigantic temple complex in Siem Reap Province in northwestern Cambodia, once the heart of an empire that stretched from South Vietnam to Laos and central Siam, is now a UNESCO World Heritage Site and the country's biggest tourist draw. Almost two million visitors descended onto the monuments in 2008. The Angkor Empire flourished between the 7th and 14th century, before it was subsumed by the aggressive policies of its stronger neighbors, and perhaps by its own delusions of grandeur.

Only in the mid-19th century did the French expedition of Henri Mouhot "rediscover" the temples for the rest of the world. Since then, the jungle that had grown over the sacred stones for centuries has slowly been stripped away, a process that continues to this day at the more remote temple locations in the province. While work on the temples halted between 1973 and 1992, mine-clearing programs and restoration projects are slowly restoring these true wonders of the world to glory; even outlying temples such as Beng Melea, which could only be reached by four-wheel-drive or helicopter a few years ago, are now easily accessible. At the same time, the Angkor ruins are beginning to show the strain of the millions of visitors and, if tourism in the area is to be sustainable, the industry will have to diversify to other more remote locations. Some of the temples may have to cap visitor numbers. For the moment though, any thought of sustainability goes against the grain of the development Siem Reap has seen in recent years.

© AROON THAEWCHATTURAT

HIGHLIGHTS

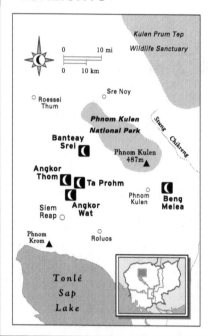

❰ Angkor Wat: The greatest of great temples, Angkor Wat is a monumental dream in stone (page 40).

❰ Angkor Thom: Cambodia's last imperial city is surrounded by a three-kilometer wall and moat. Right in its center is the Bayon, a spectacular temple dominated by towers adorned with the enigmatic smiling faces of the *bodhisattva* (page 45).

❰ Ta Prohm: The jungle-covered temple of *Tomb Raider* fame is the most romantic ruin in the Angkor Archaeological Park (page 53).

❰ Banteay Srei: This small 10th-century temple features some the most exquisite carvings of the Khmer empire (page 61).

❰ Beng Melea: Away from the crowds and subsumed by jungle, this remote temple offers visitors one of the most atmospheric experiences of any Khmer temple (page 64).

LOOK FOR ❰ TO FIND RECOMMENDED SIGHTS, ACTIVITIES, DINING, AND LODGING.

To ordinary Cambodians, Angkor symbolizes much more than the projected power of a forgotten time. Angkor is Cambodia's spiritual and economic heart. Monks and pilgrims from all over the country continue to visit the temples, especially around Khmer New Year in April. Siem Reap may appear strange to them—the formerly small market town with a couple of blocks of crumbling French colonial architecture has grown into the country's second capital—a city with more than 8,000 hotel beds, countless restaurants, souvenir shops, casinos, and bars. For those visitors who have any energy left after the temples, a number of interesting exhibitions, a couple of war museums, a pagoda with a killing field, as well as distractions such as golf courses and horse rides, could be of interest.

PLANNING YOUR TIME

If you are incredibly pressed for time, a quick one-day turn through Angkor Wat, Angkor Thom, including the Bayon, Ta Prohm, and Banteay Srei will at least give you a superficial impression of the Khmer Empire. Three days are a must for all those who want to soak up the architectural majesty of the former Angkor Empire. A week allows you to visit outlying and remote temples. Farther afield sights such as the temples Beng Melea or Koh Ker or the biosphere and floating village on the Tonlé Sap can be reached in day trips.

Siem Reap is by far the most affluent place in Cambodia and the shopping's not bad (though the markets in Phnom Penh offer a greater selection of goods at slightly better prices), which may tempt some visitors to hang around a few days longer than they'd planned.

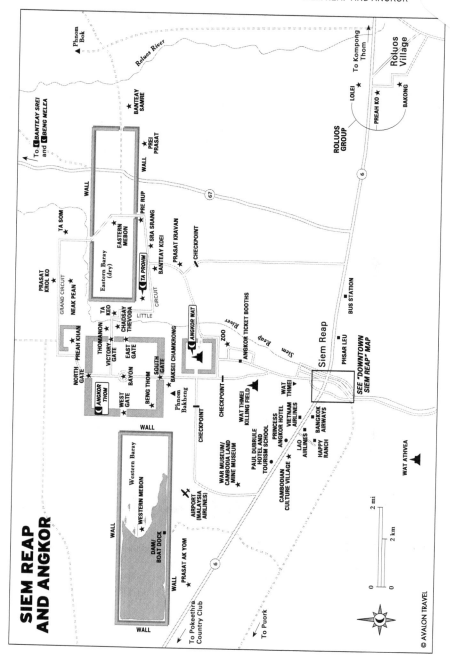

© AVALON TRAVEL

Siem Reap

The town nearest to the Angkor temples has grown from a tiny village a hundred years ago into Cambodia's second-largest city. Some locals call it the unofficial capital, thanks to the millions of tourist dollars that have been rolling in since the late 1990s. Siem Reap translates as "Defeated Thailand," a reference to the Khmer Empire at a time it controlled large swathes of Siam (today's Thailand) for several centuries. Following the sacking of Angkor by the Siamese in 1431, the tables turned and the Angkor ruins, as well as Siem Reap, were administered by Siam.

The town of Siem Reap really came into its own at the beginning of the 20th century, when the first wave of international tourists arrived. Le Grand Hotel D'Angkor opened in 1932 and tourism grew steadily until World War II. Following the war, Angkor became trendy once more and remained on the global tourist circuit until the late 1960s, when increasing turmoil in Cambodia and the neighboring war in Vietnam put an end to tourism. French archaeologists remained at the temple and tried to continue working, even as the war reached Siem Reap, but in 1975, the Khmer Rouge emptied the town and drove all its inhabitants into the countryside, where many perished. When the Vietnamese pushed the Khmer Rouge out of the government in 1979, the new occupiers put their own troops into Siem Reap. The Khmer Rouge escaped into the forests around the town and embarked on a 15-year terror campaign on Siem Reap's citizens, the Vietnamese, and, later, the United Nations Transitional Authority in Cambodia (UNTAC), which culminated in a final large-scale attack in 1993.

Today, Siem Reap is the safest city in the country and Cambodia's boomtown. In just 10 years, this sleepy backwater has turned into a thriving, chaotic metropolis. I remember the installation of Siem Reap's first traffic lights in 2001. Three policemen manned the chosen crossing, each armed with a megaphone, and spent all day explaining the traffic lights' function to passing traffic participants. At 6 P.M., the officers went home and the lights immediately became mere decoration. The traffic on the main roads is the biggest hazard around town. In 2007, the Angkor International Hospital, Cambodia's first international-standard clinic, opened—and now provides competent treatment to accident victims. Thankfully, the French town center has been tastefully restored and it's still possible to go for a quiet walk under the trees by the Siem Reap River. Many of the villages around town have lost little of their simple charm and seem barely affected by the tourist circus. Hustle, prostitution, and drugs are kept to a minimum, and if you are not looking for any trouble you are very unlikely to find any.

Siem Reap will continue to evolve and expand, and there's talk of a second airport. As long as Angkor remains one of the world's most popular archaeological sites, Siem Reap is unlikely to stop growing.

SIGHTS
The Old Market Area

Just eight years ago, the area around Old Market (Phsar Chas), right in the heart of Siem Reap and close to the river, was a run-down, dilapidated affair, a little unsavory at night. Since then, investment and restoration have taken place and the colonial buildings around the covered market have recaptured their former grace. All this makes for a francophone ambience, a nostalgic vibe with more than a whiff of l'Indochine, and a very nice space to move around in. Several downtown areas of Cambodian cities retain substantial colonial architecture, but only here has it been completely rehabilitated. The market itself has largely been given over to things tourists might buy—from DVD documentaries on the Khmer Rouge to silk scarves, rice paper prints of *apsaras*, opium pipes, and the ubiquitous *krama*, Cambodia's all-purpose head scarf. About half of the market still sells products for

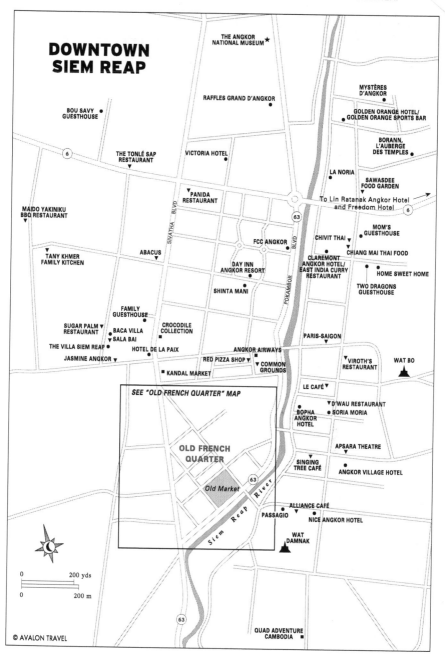

DOWNTOWN SIEM REAP

THE ANGKOR NATIONAL MUSEUM ★

MYSTÈRES D'ANGKOR ●

RAFFLES GRAND D'ANGKOR ●

GOLDEN ORANGE HOTEL/ GOLDEN ORANGE SPORTS BAR ●

BOU SAVY GUESTHOUSE ●

BORANN, L'AUBERGE DES TEMPLES ●

THE TONLÉ SAP RESTAURANT ▼

VICTORIA HOTEL ●

LA NORIA ●

SAWASDEE FOOD GARDEN

PANIDA RESTAURANT ▼

To Lin Ratanak Angkor Hotel and Freedom Hotel →

MAIDO YAKINIKU BBQ RESTAURANT ▼

MOM'S GUESTHOUSE ●

FCC ANGKOR ■

CHIVIT THAI ▼

CHIANG MAI THAI FOOD

TANY KHMER FAMILY KITCHEN

ABACUS ▼

CLAREMONT ANGKOR HOTEL/ EAST INDIA CURRY RESTAURANT

DAY INN ANGKOR RESORT ●

HOME SWEET HOME

SHINTA MANI ●

TWO DRAGONS GUESTHOUSE

FAMILY GUESTHOUSE ●

SUGAR PALM ▼ RESTAURANT

BACA VILLA ●

SALA BAI ▼

CROCODILE COLLECTION

PARIS-SAIGON ●

THE VILLA SIEM REAP ●

HOTEL DE LA PAIX ●

JASMINE ANGKOR ▼

ANGKOR AIRWAYS ●

VIROTH'S RESTAURANT ▼

WAT BO ▲

RED PIZZA SHOP ●

COMMON GROUNDS ▼

KANDAL MARKET ■

LE CAFÉ ▼

SEE "OLD FRENCH QUARTER" MAP

D'WAU RESTAURANT ▼

BOPHA ANGKOR HOTEL ●

SORIA MORIA ●

APSARA THEATRE ▼

OLD FRENCH QUARTER

SINGING TREE CAFÉ ▼

ANGKOR VILLAGE HOTEL ●

Old Market

ALLIANCE CAFÉ ●

PASSAGIO ●

NICE ANGKOR HOTEL ●

WAT DAMNAK ▲

Siem Reap River

0   200 yds
0   200 m

QUAD ADVENTURE CAMBODIA ■

© AVALON TRAVEL

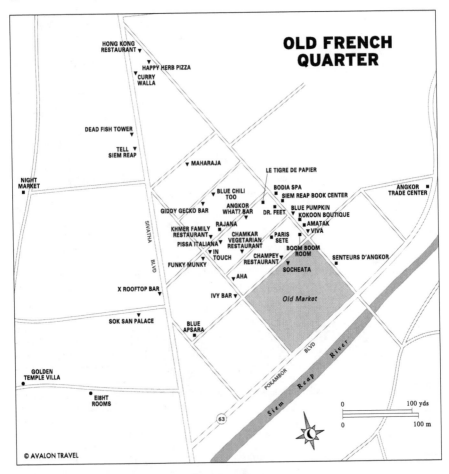

OLD FRENCH QUARTER

HONG KONG RESTAURANT ▼

HAPPY HERB PIZZA ▼

CURRY WALLA ▼

DEAD FISH TOWER ▼

TELL ▼
SIEM REAP

▼ MAHARAJA

NIGHT MARKET ■

LE TIGRE DE PAPIER

BODIA SPA ■
BLUE CHILI TOO ▼
SIEM REAP BOOK CENTER ■

ANGKOR TRADE CENTER ■

GIDDY GECKO BAR ■
ANGKOR WHAT? BAR ▼
DR. FEET ▼
BLUE PUMPKIN ▼
KOKOON BOUTIQUE

SIVATHA

KHMER FAMILY RESTAURANT ▼
RAJANA ■
CHAMKAR VEGETARIAN RESTAURANT ▼
PARIS ■
SETE
AMATAK ■
▼ VIVA

PISSA ITALIANA ▼
▼ IN TOUCH
BOOM BOOM ROOM

BLVD

FUNKY MUNKY ▼
CHAMPEY ▼
RESTAURANT ▼
SOCHEATA

SENTEURS D'ANGKOR ■

▼ AHA

X ROOFTOP BAR ▼

IVY BAR ▼

Old Market

SOK SAN PALACE ▼

BLUE APSARA ■

BLVD

POKAMBOR

Siem Reap River

GOLDEN TEMPLE VILLA ■

EIGHT ROOMS ▼

63

| 0 | | 100 yds |
| 0 | | 100 m |

© AVALON TRAVEL

the local community, including fruit, machine parts, and clothes. The streets around the market are lined with eateries (some budget, others upscale), shops, Internet cafés, and bars—making for a great stroll in the early evening. The stalls selling local products open from the crack of dawn until early evening, while the shops selling curios open around 10 A.M. and close around 7 P.M.

Wat Bo

One of the oldest temples in Siem Reap, the 18th-century Wat Bo (entrance free), on the eastern side of the river, has some interesting frescoes on the walls of the prayer hall, including the depiction of an opium-smoking Chinese trader.

Wat Damnak

Located on the eastern side of the river, this large temple compound (entrance free) was once a royal palace and has been beautifully restored. In the afternoons, locals come to sit by a large stone basin filled with lotus flowers and catfish. The Center of Khmer Studies is located in a handsome building dating back

Wat Athvea, a small Angkor-era temple, is in a village between Siem Reap and Phnom Krom.

to the early 20th century, located within the temple compound.

Wat Athvea

Wat Athvea (entrance free) is a very special place. The active monastery lies in the shade of a bamboo grove, right next door to a small, but very handsome and well-preserved Angkor-era temple. The pagoda is never empty—monks, village elders, and musicians can usually be found in the prayer hall. An open reception hall and a prayer hall, as well as wooden huts that serve as accommodation for the monks, make up the compound. In the prayer hall, hundreds of Buddha statues are gathered around a central shrine and the walls are covered in frescoes depicting the life of the Buddha. Once a year, during Khmer New Year, all the statues are washed by the local community, a ceremony that entails a wild water battle.

The 12th-century temple next door, surrounded by a high laterite wall, is often deserted, although local people conduct merit-making ceremonies in its single main tower.

Wat Athvea is a great place to gain an impression of what the atmosphere around the temples was like before tourists rediscovered Angkor. Just a few minutes away from Cambodia's busiest shopping streets, an incredibly peaceful and relaxed ambience pervades the temple buildings. The two buildings are off the main road between Siem Reap and Phnom Krom. The turn-off to the temple is marked by a large gate on the right-hand side, about four kilometers south of Phsar Chas (Old Market). It's not necessary to have a pass for Angkor to visit this ruin.

Beyond the temples, a small village—with traditional family homes on stilts—is full of friendly teenagers keen to take visitors around the area. Some of the kids speak English fairly well and have a few facts about temple and country life ready, but don't expect a real "tour." It's the experience rather than the facts that counts here. A donation of a few dollars for the young guides is expected.

Wat Thmei Killing Field

Although the Khmer Rouge never dared to attack the temple ruins of Angkor, many people died in the area during and after the communist reign. Siem Reap Province contains numerous killing fields. Wat Thmei (entrance free), an active temple on a side road from Siem Reap to Angkor, has a glass-paneled stupa in its courtyard, which is filled with the bones of victims of the Khmer Rouge.

The Angkor National Museum

The Angkor National Museum (tel. 063/966601, www.angkornationalmuseum. com, daily 9 A.M.–7 P.M.), on the road to the temples, just beyond the Le Grand Hotel d'Angkor, opened in late 2007 and serves as a light introduction to the magic of the Angkorian Empire. Visitors to this massive complex, a project run by a private company in conjunction with the Cambodian Ministry of Culture and Fine Arts, will be left wondering whether they are in a shopping mall or a museum, but that's not to say that a visit is a waste of time. Several exhibition galleries on Khmer civilization, Angkor Wat, and Angkor Thom contain some fine examples of Angkorian artifacts and statues. A number of rooms equipped with comfortable seating show short, informative movies in nine different languages. Audio tours of the entire facility are also available. The pieces on show come from the storage of the National Museum in Phnom Penh and from Conservation d'Angkor. A highlight is the Hall of a Thousand Buddhas, which is very nicely lit and does indeed contain 1,000 Buddha statues. A dome with a giant screen split into three parts almost delivers an IMAX experience. Contemporary artists also find a space here, with regular exhibitions related to Angkor held in a smaller domed hall inside the museum. The museum's exit leads straight into a souvenir shop.

All in all, the number of artifacts is a bit light, but the museum is still finding its feet and, anyway, this is edutainment. It doesn't compare to the National Museum in Phnom Penh, but it isn't trying to. The only real criticism is the ticket price: US$12 for foreigners, US$3 for Khmer.

The Cambodian Cultural Village

This rather unsophisticated theme park (tel. 063/963836, www.cambodianculturalvillage. com, daily 9 A.M.–9 P.M.), located on the airport road, whisks visitors through Cambodia's turbulent history. Exhibits include replicas of temples, miniature versions of entire villages (including a so-called millionaire house, "a place where ancient rich men stayed") as well as life-size re-creations of scenes from Cambodia's past. Traditional dance performances from around the country take place at several locations in the village. Check the website for times. The place made headlines in 2003 when a display illustrating the presence of UNTAC in the country was limited to a foreign soldier embracing a Khmer sex worker. That particular item has been removed, but the US$11 entrance fee for foreigners is still not entirely justified.

The War Museum and the Cambodia Land Mine Museum

Two museums remind visitors of the 30 years of war in the latter half of the 20th century and the legacy of conflict that Cambodia has endured. The War Museum (no phone, daily 9 A.M.–5 P.M., US$1), built and managed by the Department of Defense, is close to town, just north of Route 6 towards the airport. The official ad reads, original spelling intact, "The War Museum is very unique, all kinds of old weapons used during almost 3 decades of wars in Cambodia. Tanks, Armored Personal Carrier, Artilleries, Mortars, Land mines and small arms…etc. So you spend just thirty minutes or 1 hour. You'll see all these weapons."

The museum is not dedicated to any specific conflict, nor, it seems, are its planners aware of any chronological relevance of recent warfare on Cambodian soil supposedly illustrated here. Tanks, mortars, and anti-aircraft guns rust in the sun, while a dilapidated collection of firearms is kept in an open shed. Some of the weaponry on show was manufactured as early as the 1930s and hails from places as diverse as Vietnam, China, the Soviet Union, and East Germany. There are mock mine fields and a large collection of landmines remind visitors of the continuing scourge of these weapons in Cambodia.

The Aki Ra Mine Action Museum (tel. 012/598951, www.cambodialandminemuseum.org, daily 7:30 A.M.–5:30 P.M., US$1), also called the Cambodia Land Mine Museum Relief Facility, is managed by a Canadian NGO. It's located out near Banteay Srei, and is best visited during a trip to this outlying temple. There's information on land mines and a large collection of war scrap dug up from the surrounding countryside, and visitors can challenge themselves by walking through a mock mine field and booby traps.

ENTERTAINMENT AND EVENTS

There are plenty of nighttime hangouts competing for those who still have some energy left at the end of the day. Bars-cum-restaurants are in the majority, and a couple of venues offer live music. The suspect ambience so typical of many of Phnom Penh's bars and clubs is virtually nonexistent in Siem Reap. For those in search of some traditional entertainment, *apsara* dance performances are put on by several upscale hotels and numerous restaurants. And there's always the Night Market, with its bar and food court.

Bars and Clubs

BARS

Right in the heart of old Siem Reap, Pub Street offers some appealing venues. Restaurants, bars, and clubs line this narrow road; street vendors sell anything they can think of; and the atmosphere is safe and relaxed. Best of all, the police cordon the area off at night, so there's no motorized traffic to worry about, should you stumble onto the street at 2 A.M.

Not as old as the temples, but open for business since 1998, the **Angkor What? Bar** (daily 5 P.M.–very late) has grown from a hole-in-the-wall late-night filling station with a beer-spattered pool table into a much larger, spacey affair—every inch of wall space is covered in guests' signatures. Join the club. Tables out

front are a perfect vantage point to survey the action on the street.

Reassuringly pop-tastic, both in name and character, is the Western-style **Funky Munky** (www.funkymunkycambodia.com, noon–very late except on Mon.) on Pub Street, which spins contemporary dance tunes and serves a wide range of cocktails late into the night. The **Blue Chili Too** (daily 6 P.M.–2 A.M.), located in a narrow alley behind Pub Street, is Siem Reap's gay-friendly nighttime hangout. It follows the same concept as its brother operation in Phnom Penh: soft lighting, nice decor, and company.

The **Ivy Bar** (daily 7 A.M.–very late), on the southwestern corner of the Old Market area, has been around for years and remains a good meeting spot. Its claim to fame is Pol Pot's toilet seat, spirited away from Brother Number 1's last home in Anlong Veng in 2000, and now proudly displayed in a frame on the wall, offset by some of Gordon Sharpless' enigmatic Cambodia images and a pool table. The pub food and breakfasts, both Western and Asian, are not bad either. The **Giddy Gecko Bar** (daily 5 P.M.–very late) is located on the first floor of a corner building in the Old Market area, hence offering great views over the nighttime action in the heart of Siem Reap. It's a laid-back place where you can sip a cocktail, surf your laptop with Wi-Fi access, or smoke a hookah.

In the forecourt of the Golden Orange Hotel in the Wat Bo area, across the river from the Old Market, the friendly **Golden Orange Sports Bar** (daily 6 P.M.–midnight) is a small island of Americana. Hotel guests and visitors can relax to music familiar to American ears (anything from The Rolling Stones to the Carpenters), enjoy a free game of pool, drink a cold beer, surf the Internet, and watch Hollywood movies, all at the same time if necessary.

NIGHTCLUBS

Siem Reap's premier nightclub suitable for tourists (there are quite a few very rowdy Khmer clubs around as well) is the **Sok San Palace,** which plays house, R&B, hip hop, and funk. It serves drinks that aren't overpriced and features laser lighting, dancing girls, and karaoke rooms. The club is located in central Siem Reap, on a side street off Sivatha Boulevard, a little south of X Bar.

LIVE MUSIC

A cross between an American roadhouse bar and a Thai beer hall (the owner is Thai), the eclectic and huge **Dead Fish Tower,** located in the heart of town on Sivatha Boulevard, provides seating on three levels with a small stage on the first level. Traditional dance performances and live bands are featured regularly and the steaks are pretty good (US$6–12). Their advertising reads "We don't serve Dog, Cat, Rat or Worm," though there's a page on the menu entitled "Scary Dishes" (with pig's heart, eel, and frogs, for example). Most diners are impressed by the crocodile pit on the way to the restrooms. A plate of fish to feed the large and very much alive reptiles is just US$0.50, and the jaded creatures start snapping their jaws as soon as you raise your arm above them. This is the perfect place to get rid of those pesky travel companions you have been trying to shake for a week.

In Touch (daily 11 A.M.–2 A.M.), a bar-cum-restaurant serving Thai food, located amongst the bustle of Pub Street, hosts live cover bands (mostly light jazz) upstairs from 9 P.M.

Performing Arts

Many of the upscale hotels in town put on traditional Khmer dance performances during their dinners. These usually include both classical and folk dances and tend to last about an hour. One of the most professional troupes works the *apsara* dance on the Apsara Terrace at the **Raffles Grand Hotel d'Angkor** (tel. 063/963888). Dinner performances run Mondays, Wednesdays, and Fridays at 7:45 P.M. from October to May and it's US$32 a head. Other similarly sumptuous dinner events can be attended at the **Sofitel Royal Angkor** (tel. 063/964600), on the road to the temples and the **Victoria Angkor** (tel. 063/760428).

Outside the high-end hotels, the **Apsara**

Theatre (tel. 063/963561), a massive wooden Khmer-style auditorium, is probably your best bet to see cultural dances in Siem Reap; it's located in the Wat Bo area, opposite the Angkor Village Hotel. Traditional *apsara* dance performances take place on Tuesdays, Thursdays, and Saturdays 7–9 P.M. with a set menu Khmer dinner. Dinner and performance are US$22. The **Tonlé Sap Restaurant** on the airport road is really a package tour affair, with buffet dinners including a traditional dance performance for US$12. Shows start at 7:30 P.M. From 7–9 P.M., performances by a Khmer dancer are also held at the **Dead Fish Tower** on Sivatha Boulevard, but they tend to be subsumed within the venue's youthful, cosmopolitan atmosphere.

Traditional Cambodian shadow puppet theater (Speik Thom and Speik Toot), featuring stories from the *Reamker,* the Khmer version of the Indian epic the *Ramayana,* as well as popular folk stories can be seen at the hotel **La Noria** (tel. 063/964242) on the eastern side of the river on Wednesdays (7–9 P.M.) and at the **Butterflies Garden Restaurant** (tel. 063/761211, www.butterfliesofangkor.com), on the road to the airport. For the latter venue's schedules, check the website.

With his weekly solo cello performances and talks, **Beatocello** (www.beatocello.com), or Dr. Beat Richner, raises much-needed funds for the Jayavarman VII Hospital in Siem Reap and the Kantha Bopha 1 and 2 Children's Hospitals in Phnom Penh. Shows take place every Saturday at 7:15 P.M. at the Jayavarman VII Hospital on the road to the Angkor ruins. Entrance is free, but a donation is appropriate. In the day time, the Jayavarman VII Hospital also welcomes blood donations. On Tuesdays and Thursdays, a film about Dr. Beat Richner, entitled *Doctor Beat and the Passive Genocide of Children* is shown at 7:15 P.M. at the Jayavarman VII Hospital. Entrance is free.

Art Galleries

One of the smartest galleries–cum–drinking dens in Siem Reap is the spacious retro-futuristic **Arts Lounge** in the Hotel de la Paix. Regular exhibition of traditional and

HEAVENLY *APSARAS:*
THE KHMER NATIONAL BALLET

Khmer ballet, or classical dance, is one of three categories of Cambodian dance (the others being folk and vernacular dance). Originally the ballet was performed exclusively for the royal court. With independence from France, classical dance was introduced to the Cambodian public to celebrate Khmer culture. During the Khmer Rouge years, the art form was almost lost, but since the early 1990s, the School of Fine Arts in Phnom Penh has been training new batches of dancers. The dancers, all female, have to learn more than 3,500 movements, each of which has its own specific meaning, often symbolizing aspects of nature, such as the opening of a flower. Students are trained for 9 or 12 years to learn the intricate positions and movements the dances entail. Other dances tell the story of Cambodia's origins, a union between a hermit named Kampu and a woman called Apsara Mera. The dancing *apsaras,* who grace many temple walls, suggest that the royal ballet was most popular in the 10th to 12th centuries. The School of Fine Arts shows off the results of their endurance training on special occasions such as during Khmer New Year in front of Angkor Wat.

Since mass tourism has arrived in Cambodia in recent years, many hotels and restaurants in Siem Reap and Phnom Penh offer Khmer classical dance performances as a dinner accompaniment. One of the best places to catch a high-quality performance is the Grand Hotel d'Angkor in Siem Reap.

---

contemporary Cambodian artists are presented here at monthly intervals. The **Red Gallery** (www.redgalleryasia.com), on the premises of the FCC Angkor, promotes and exhibits paintings and sculptures by some of Cambodia's most established international and local artists in a relaxed and intimate environment. Exhibits change every now and then, and the quality of the work is consistently high. Drop by for insight into a slowly emerging contemporary Cambodian art aesthetic.

The **McDermott Gallery** (www.mcdermottgallery.com), located next to AHA in The Passage by the Old Market is one of the most attractive exhibition spaces in Cambodia and features fine art photography from a number of well-established as well as emerging artists. It's well worth a visit. A second McDermott Gallery can be found on the property of FCC Angkor. Here, photographer John McDermott exhibits his otherworldly and idiosyncratic infrared black-and-white photographs of the Angkor ruins. Large prints retail US$450–3,000.

Another enigmatic photographer, the Italian Pierre Poretti, exhibits his work at the **Klick Gallery** (www.iklektik.com/photography) located in The Passage by the Old Market. Poretti shoots in black and white and then hand-tints his images. His series of photographs of the Angkor ruins have a nostalgic look. Other series include pictures from Bali, Myanmar, Vietnam, and Laos, as well as portraits of Grace Jones.

Stephane Delapree, a French-Canadian cartoonist, paints extremely colorful naive canvasses of Cambodian scenes. The artist calls his work Happy Paintings (www.happypainting.net) and he has a gallery called **Happy Cambodia** in the Old Market area, as well as another branch in Phnom Penh.

Cultural Events and Festivals
KHMER NEW YEAR
During Khmer New Year, which falls in April, be prepared to share Angkor with thousands of celebrating Cambodians, who travel from all over the country to picnic and celebrate amongst the ruins.

THE ANGKOR PHOTO FESTIVAL
The Angkor Photo Festival (www.photographyforchange.net) was created in 2005 and

now draws both famous and passionate photographers from around the world to Siem Reap in November each year. Outdoor projections showcase regional and international photographers in different locations in Siem Reap.

The festival also has social goals. During their stay, well-established photographers from all over the world will tutor free workshops for emerging Asian shooters and the festival will also present its outreach programs for vulnerable people.

SHOPPING
Markets
Old Market, known to the locals as Phsar Chas, has become more commercial since visitor numbers really picked up in 2003, but this most traditional of Siem Reap markets is still divided down the middle into stalls selling curios and souvenirs and, across a central courtyard alive with vegetable vendors, stalls that sell household goods and cheap electronics to local people. Along its western side, a number of well-priced Khmer restaurants cater both to foreign visitors and Cambodians. The area around the market is lined with boutiques selling handicrafts, often produced by underprivileged and marginalized people.

Kandal Market, in English Center Market, is Siem Reap's largest market hall, squarely aimed at foreign souvenir hunters. Besides fine silks and clothing, it sells every type of tack imaginable, much of it brought in from neighboring countries. Haggle for everything and don't be surprised when the only other customers in here are tour groups.

The **Night Market** (www.angkornightmarket.com), opened in 2007 in its own little compound a few minutes' walk to the west of the Old Market area. A huge collection of stalls selling silks, handicrafts, and curios—many of them imported from neighboring countries—is on display. Orphans and people with disabilities get stalls at a discount and NGOs also exhibit and sell their products here, but most of what you'll see are generic souvenirs. Several movies about aspects of Cambodian history are shown nightly. A food court (not always open)

and a bar will keep you fuelled up in between browsing silks, bootleg DVDs, or jewelry. The market opens daily at 4 P.M., and stalls remain open till midnight.

Shopping Mall
Siem Reap's first shopping mall, the **Angkor Trade Center,** located just by the river a little north of the Old Market area, is a rather modest creation, with branches of Swensen's and the Pizza Company (as well as a small supermarket) on the ground floor and a cheap food court on the second floor. In between, stalls sell bootleg DVDs and clothes.

Craft and Book Shops
A number of fashionable boutiques are located in the Old Market area. These outlets have fixed prices and are not cheap, but you will find items here not available in the markets. **Senteurs d'Angkor** sells spices, tea, coffee, soaps, oils, and Khmer wine, as well as silks. Very similar yet different is **Kokoon Boutique,** which sells some pottery as well as silks and home decoration items. **Amatak** sells handprinted T-shirts, hats, and silks. The NGO-based **Rajana,** on Sivatha Boulevard, sells articles made from wood, as well as silks and other handmade souvenirs. More on the noisy and youthful side is the **Boom Boom Room,** also near the Old Market, where you can upload a vast range of music to your iPod or any MP3 player at a fraction of its original retail price. Similar outlets exist in Phnom Penh and Sihanoukville. Besides music, trendy club wear and drinks are for sale.

The **Crocodile Collection** on Sivatha Boulevard sells reptilian belts, shoes, and wallets, not just made of crocodile leather, but also of stingray, cobra, and ostrich leather. A little army of stuffed crocs welcomes visitors at the door. A croc wallet is around US$100. One would assume that the crocodile and ostrich leather is derived from animals bred specifically for this purpose. Cobras and stingrays are much more likely to be caught in the wild.

Numerous mobile book vendors, many

of them maimed by land mines, move through the Old Market area and usually carry a selection of nonfiction titles about Cambodia. Inside the Old Market, several book stalls carry the same limited choice. For a wide selection of books, some genuine, some pirated, including a whole shelf full of American underground writers, as well as bestsellers, classics, travel guides, and nonfiction on Cambodia, Vietnam, and Laos, head to **Blue Apsara.** This shop just south of the Old Market area is probably Siem Reap's best-stocked secondhand bookstore. **Monument Books** at the FCC Shopping Plaza sells new books, but they come at a high price. There's a second branch at the airport. The **Siem Reap Book Center** near the Old Market looks like an old trader's shop in India and sells a decent selection of history and photo books, as well as stationary, office supplies, countless souvenirs of doubtful taste, and chocolate bars.

A curious and incongruous outlet to hang around in is **Paris Sete** on Pub Street. This French shop specializes in beautiful if expensive lacquer images of Tintin cartoons and Expressionist art, imported from Saigon. The collection of photos and postcards on sale—including recruitment posters for the French colonial efforts of the 20th century—is worth perusing, and browsers may even find a couple of original rare books, posters, and artifacts.

SPORTS AND RECREATION
Swimming
While bathing in the river that runs through Siem Reap is not recommended, a few hotel pools open to outsiders and can offer some respite from the heat. The largest pools in town can be found at the **Princess Angkor Hotel** (tel. 063/760056, www.princessangkor.com) on the road to the airport; the **Lin Ratanak Angkor Hotel** (tel. 063/969888, www.lin-ratanakangkor.com), behind Phsar Samaki off Route 6; and the **Raffles Grand Hotel d'Angkor** (tel. 063/963888, www.raffles.com/en_ra/property/rga) in the heart of town.

Cycling
As foreigners are no longer allowed to drive their own motorized vehicles around Siem Reap or Angkor, the only alternative for visitors determined to see the area on their own terms is pedal power. Please note that while the roads around the temples are pretty flat, it does get very hot on the long stretches where the tree cover has been cut. Bring sun protection and drink plenty of water. Bicycles can be rented from guesthouses at US$2–3 a day.

Golf
The closest 18-hole golf course to Siem Reap is the Nick Faldo–designed **Angkor Golf Resort** (tel. 063/392288, www.angkor-golf.com), just six kilometers from the city along the road to the airport. A second professional-standard course, the **Pokeethra Country Club** (tel. 063/964600, www.pokeethra.com) lies some 16 kilometers from Siem Reap on Route 6. This 18-hole course, complete with driving range, restaurant, and pro-shop, is managed by Sofitel.

Cooking School
Le Tigre de Papier (tel. 063/760930, www.le-tigredepapier.com), a restaurant on Pub Street, offers half-day introductions to the Cambodian kitchen. The course (US$12) includes a trip to Old Market (Phsar Chas) to purchase ingredients and two hours of supervised preparations, including both cooking and food presentation. Participants get to check out each other's creations at lunch.

Horseback Riding
For avid riders, countryside horse trails can be explored from **Happy Ranch** (tel. 012/920002, www.thehappyranch.com), located a couple of kilometers from downtown Siem Reap. Rides are US$18 an hour, or US$31 for two hours. Group lessons are US$18 per student, one-on-lessons are US$22. Riders must weigh less than 90 kilograms (200 pounds).

Quad Bike Tours
If you fancy racing a quad car through the Cambodian countryside, then look no

further than **Quad Adventure Cambodia** (tel. 017/784-727, www.quad-adventure-cambodia. com), located on the eastern side of the river, not far from Wat Damnak. Different tour packages on American-made Polaris Trail Boss quads are available, from two-hour romps to longer full-day trips to remote corners of the province.

Massage and Spas

Many of the upscale hotels and resorts in Siem Reap have their own spas or massage services. Outside of the hotel scene, head for **Bodia Spa** (www.bodia-spa.com), which includes a fashionable boutique and café. Bodia is located right next to U-Care Pharmacy in the Old Market area. **Islands Massage** (body massage US$8/hr) and **BE VIP Massage** (body massage US$6/hr), a few doors down, and **Dr. Feet** (foot reflexology US$6/hr), across the road, are all respectable.

ACCOMMODATIONS
Under US$15

One of the most reliable cheapies in town, though a bit off the beaten track, is the friendly **(Bou Savy Guesthouse** (tel. 063/964967, www.bousavyguesthouse.com, US$9 without a/c, US$15 with a/c), located on a garden property in a small lane just past Wat Kesararam on Route 6. The Khmer family who owns this place has a hands-on management policy, which translates into simple but clean rooms, personable, caring service, and all the usual travel and tour programs. All rooms have en-suite bathrooms and TV.

The **Baca Villa** (tel. 063/965328, www.baca-villa.com, US$8 without a/c, US$15 with a/c) is a good budget option on Taphul Road. The en-suite rooms are nothing to write home about, but they are clean, large enough, and have a TV. The guesthouse has a good garden restaurant that serves a large selection of Cambodian dishes, as well as backpacker fare, and organizes its own bike and four-wheel-drive tours.

Another rock-bottom place is the **Family Guesthouse** (tel. 092/968960, familyguesthouse@gmail.com, US$6 without a/c, US$13

with a/c), located on a small side street off Sivatha Boulevard, a hundred meters north of Kandal Market. The small, clean rooms are a steal, though they have few amenities. There's Wi-Fi and a decent rooftop restaurant.

Located on a quiet side street in the Wat Bo area, **Home Sweet Home** (tel. 012/824626, www.homesweethomeangkor.com, US$6 without a/c, US$12 with a/c) might not have any great thrills, but it's a good value. The decent-size rooms are clean, and have en-suite baths and TV and either fans or air-conditioning. Should you be bored or burnt out on CNN, BBC, and HBO, or simply require more high-brow entertainment, it's possible to rent DVD players and movies for US$2. The Internet service downstairs in the restaurant is free for guests. This guesthouse, like most operations of its size, also offers a travel and visa service and laundry.

The **Nice Angkor Hotel** (tel. 063/966247, www.niceangkor.com, US$15) is really quite nice, just as the name suggests. This bargain basement guesthouse, located on the eastern side of the river, not too far from the Old Market, offers clean and simple air-conditioned rooms, most with their own small balconies (though not the rooms on the ground floor, of course). Guests can access the Internet free of charge and the restaurant serves Khmer and international standards.

US$15-25

If you are looking for a good mid-range guesthouse with great service, check out the **(Two Dragons Guesthouse** (tel. 063/965107, http://talesofasia.com/cambodia-twodragons.htm, US$17–27), near Wat Po. The Two Dragons offers 13 spotless if small rooms and is fronted by a restaurant that turns out good Thai dishes. The main reason to stay here, however, is the establishment's owner, American writer/photographer and tireless pundit Gordon Sharpless, whose website, http://talesofasia. com, has been informing Cambodia travelers about the state of the roads, the temples, and the country for many years. Needless to say, the Two Dragons is a mine of information and

Gordon's photo-portraits of life in Cambodia are not bad either. There's free Wi-Fi access and a no-smoking policy in the rooms.

Not far away, but on the noisier Wat Bo Road is **Mom's Guesthouse** (tel. 012/630170, www.momguesthouse.com), which was once located in a traditional wooden building, but moved into a more swanky, newly built townhouse in 2007. Mom has decent sized but slightly dark air-conditioned rooms for US$20 including breakfast, or brighter deluxe rooms for the same price, but excluding the breakfast. The guesthouse offers all the usual travel services and has an ATM on the premises.

A stylish and low-cost accommodation option is the youthful and trendy **Ei8ht Rooms** (tel. 063/969788, www.ei8htrooms. com, US$16–22), located in two buildings on opposite sides of a side street off Sivatha Boulevard to the south of the Old Market area. Both common areas and the spacious air-conditioned rooms are carefully decorated with silks and black and white furniture. All rooms come with DVD players and a large selection of movies free of charge. Internet access in the lobby is free for guests. Several grass-roof pavilions on the roof make for a nice spot to watch the sun go down.

Golden Temple Villa (tel. 012/943459, www.goldentemplevilla.com, US$8–30), on the same lane as Ei8ht Rooms, is an orange-themed building, and both the outside and inside sport a uniform color tone. It's located in a luscious garden, overgrown with fully grown bamboo clusters. The 40 smallish rooms (all en-suite with tubs) are clean and smartly kept with silk curtains around the beds. Some rooms have air-conditioning, some have balconies. Downstairs, there's free Internet service for guests and the restaurant serves typical Khmer and Western dishes.

US$25-50

On the east side of the river, not far from Wat Bo, the **Bopha Angkor Hotel** (tel. 063/964928, www.bopha-angkor.com, US$38–58) offers smart and stylish rooms with traditional decor; some rooms have private balconies. The

attractive restaurant, serving mostly Khmer dishes, is popular, even with people who don't stay here. Try the excellent dim sum breakfast (US$3.50). A decent-sized pool will help weary temple visitors relax.

Anonymous but clean and spacious air-conditioned rooms welcome guests at the friendly and helpful **Freedom Hotel** (tel. 063/963473, www.freedomhotel.info, US$15–50), which has a very nice pool and a gym. Located on Route 6, west of Phsar Leu, this large budget place also has its own silk outlet.

French-owned **La Noria** (tel. 063/964242, www.lanoriaangkor.com, US$29–39), near Wat Bo Lanka, offers small but smart air-conditioned rooms decorated with traditional Khmer handicrafts in two-story bungalows, located around a small pool in a luscious garden. The poolside bar might just be the thing after a day at the temples. Alternatively you could avail yourself to a massage treatment on the premises. Following the same concept as La Noria, the smart two-story boutique bungalows set in a lush open garden promise a pleasant stay at the friendly **Borann, l'Auberge des Temples** (tel. 063/964740, www.borann. com, US$33, or US$44 with balcony), which is located off Wat Bo Road. Each good-size, en-suite, air-conditioned room (four per bungalow) is carefully designed with (partly antique) redwood furniture and cow-hide shadow puppets from the *Reamker,* and opens onto a private terrace. The in-house restaurant serves light Khmer and Western dishes, with main courses around US$6. And there's a pool.

The **Paul Dubrule Hotel and Tourism School** (tel. 063/963672, www.ecolepauldu-brule.org, US$25–50), way out on the road to the airport, is not really a hotel at all, but Siem Reap's first school training young and underprivileged Cambodians in the arts of the hotel business. The school turns out about 100 students a year, most of whom find work in the industry. Best of all, the school has four beautifully and individually designed rooms, each one donated by a different five-star hotel. These rooms are used for training purposes, hence the low rates. If you don't mind staying a little farther from the action, you can enjoy first-class international facilities at a budget price and get the chance to observe this commendable school close-up. During term time, from October to July, **Le Jardin des Delices,** an adjacent restaurant, serves the creations of the trainee cooks. The school also offers half-day upscale cooking classes.

(€ The Villa Siem Reap (tel. 063/761036, www.thevillasiemreap.com, US$15–40), located on Thapul Road a few minutes' walk from the Old Market area, is something of a concept guesthouse; itt makes the most of its budget facilities and offers simple air-conditioned rooms with brilliant purple color schemes. All rooms have Wi-Fi, the restaurant downstairs has an agreeable atmosphere and dishes from around US$5, and guests have free use of the large swimming pool at the Princess Angkor Hotel on Route 6. The staff is young and friendly and the whole place exudes positive energy. Highly recommended and a bargain to boot are the eco-tours that the guesthouse offers, especially the trips to Beng Melea, tours through Cambodian villages that take several NGOs and their activities on board, as well as trips on the Tonlé Sap that protect visitors from the money-making operations that control access to the lake villages. Groups are small (maximum eight people) and always accompanied by an experienced English-speaking guide. Participants can teach English at a local school, partake in the rice harvest, or try the local rice wine.

A modest but smart choice is the very neat and Swiss-German managed **Passagio** (tel. 063/964732, www.passagio-hotel.com, US$30 including breakfast), just north of Wat Damnak on the eastern side of the river. Spacious and spotless air-conditioned rooms with tasteful decor and furnishings, TV, and en-suite hot water are located in a modern townhouse surrounded by a small garden. A small pool gives you a chance to cool off after a long day amongst the ruins. The restaurant serves Khmer cuisine and international favorites with a Swiss leaning—Cordon Bleu is US$8.50.

The recommended **(€ Golden Orange Hotel** (tel. 063/965389, www.goldenorange-hotel.com, US$25 including breakfast), located in the Wat Po Lanka area, is run by Doug, a somewhat abrasive but friendly American, and offers nicely turned-out, spotless, international-standard air-conditioned rooms. Some rooms have Jacuzzi-style bath tubs, just the thing after a long day visiting the temples. Broadband LAN and Wi-Fi Internet access, a restaurant serving Asian and Western food, a roof-top terrace with a great view across parts of Siem Reap, and all the usual services—such as tours, ticket service, and even a sports bar with a pool table—round out the picture. You bet!

US$50-100

Located behind Wat Po Lanka, the quiet, very private and francophone **Mystères d'Angkor** (tel. 063/963639, www.mysteres-angkor.com, US$49–74) has handsome wood and stone air-conditioned pavilions (four rooms to a building) around a small swimming pool set in a wonderful tropical garden, complete with mango trees and coconut palms. The rooms are bright and beautifully furnished with traditional rosewood furniture. The main building houses the reception area, a pool table, and an excellent restaurant that serves mostly Khmer dishes. A set-menu dinner is US$8.50.

The four-story boutique hotel **Soria Moria** (tel. 063/964768, www.thesoriamoria.com, US$45–90) is located in the Wat Bo area and offers large and bright, air-conditioned European-style rooms with carefully selected furnishings, TV, Wi-Fi, and minibar. The in-house fusion restaurant serves Scandinavian and Japanese cuisine. On Wednesdays, from 5 P.M.–10 P.M., all dishes and drinks cost just US$1. The rooftop bar, with a whirlpool tub, is a good place to relax in the evenings. Spa treatment is also available. An *apsara* dance show, organized by the Sankheum Center for Children (www.sangkheum.org), takes place every night and is free for guests, though donations to the NGO are appreciated.

The **Lin Ratanak Angkor Hotel** (tel. 063/969888, www.linratanakangkor.com,

US$60–120), behind Phsar Samaki off Route 6, is a typical upscale Cambodian hotel offering medium-size, spotless, carpeted rooms with en-suite bathrooms, TV, minibar, air-conditioning, and Wi-Fi. One of the main advantages of this hotel is the larger-than-average swimming pool. The restaurant serves Western and Khmer standards. Breakfast is included in the room price and children under 12 are free.

The **Day Inn Angkor Resort** (tel. 063/760503, www.dayinnangkor.com, US$90) is a smart mid-range colonial-style hotel right in the heart of Siem Reap behind the post office. Large, attractive, air-conditioned rooms with tropical rattan furnishings are located around a large pool. Rates include breakfast.

A good mid-range option in the Wat Bo area is the **Claremont Angkor Hotel** (tel. 063/966898, www.claremontangkor.com), an Australian-owned place that offers smart, good-sized rooms with a cool ambience and real bathtubs. Doubles cost around US$70 for walk-ins, or US$55 if you book over the Internet. Guests also have the use of a fully functional gym, a small swimming pool, and Internet, and there's an in-house Indian restaurant on the sixth floor.

US$100-200

Located next to Siem Reap's Royal Residence, the **Foreign Correspondents Club Angkor (FCC Angkor)** (tel. 063/760280, www.fcccambodia.com, US$170 garden view, US$150 pool view) is not a media hangout as one might suspect, but this smart boutique hotel and restaurant does follow the same philosophical and aesthetic concept as the original FCC in Phnom Penh. The rooms are of modest size but feature a real sense of planning and carefully arranged decor and have a cosmopolitan international boutique feel. Expect attractive bathrooms. The small saltwater pool is a welcome break from the heat and there's an in-house spa.

There are countless mid-range and upscale hotels on the road to the airport catering to tour groups—many of them run-down after less than a decade in service. One of the best

of these massive complexes is the **Princess Angkor Hotel** (tel. 063/760056, www.princessangkor.com, US$100–120 rooms, US$180 suites), which offers international-standard but fairly anonymous, spacious rooms and suites with thick carpets—all with air-conditioning, TV, minibar, and complimentary tea, coffee, and water. Guests can also avail themselves of massage services and a gym. The real advantage of this hotel over many of its neighbors is its large swimming pool. Oh, and there's a casino attached.

A unique hotel experience is the **Angkor Village Hotel** (tel. 063/963561, www.angkorvillage.com, US$109–199) in the Wat Bo area. This collection of traditional Khmer wooden stilt houses is set in a beautiful, spacious, jungle-like garden compound with fully grown rain-trees, coconut palms, banana plants, and bamboo clusters. The wooden houses all feature en-suite bathrooms, air-conditioning, TV, and Internet access, and there's a swimming pool.

The **Shinta Mani** (tel. 063/761998, www.shintamani.com, US$100–140), which looks a bit like a Cambodian government building, is just around the corner from the post office. It's a small and pleasant upscale hotel, with just 18 spacious, tastefully furnished, air-conditioned rooms, located in cool whitewashed galleries around a medium-size swimming pool (US$5 for nonguests). Internet service is available in the lobby area. This hotel is connected to the Institute of Hospitality, a school teaching Western culinary skills to local youngsters. The students get a small stipend and virtually all participants find work in the industry after completing their nine-month course. The attached spa offers massages, body scrubs, therapeutic facials, and hand and foot care.

If you can do without total authenticity, but will enjoy the best possible copy of something that never really existed—namely the colonial paradise—then the **Victoria Hotel** (tel. 063/760428, www.victoriahotels-asia.com), just to the west of the Royal Independence Gardens, will fulfill your expectations. Located in a massive colonial-style compound designed with a great eye for detail, this French-owned property might only be five years old, but conveys all the nostalgia you will need. The airy reception area is invitingly intimate and yet formal, and the rooms (all with air-conditioning, TV, minibar, LAN and Wi-Fi, and private balcony, US$115–125) are furnished with perfect copies of sumptuous period furniture. The spacious suites (US$330) have all been designed to individual concepts—such as the Maharajah Suite and Governor Suite, each with their personal color schemes and decor. The steel cage elevators add a nice touch and there's a good-size swimming pool in a central courtyard. Best of all, guests may choose to be driven around the temples in vintage Citroëns—now that's hard to beat for a classy way to see the wonders of Angkor.

Over US$200

For the ultimate colonial-era experience in Siem Reap, look no further than the historic **Raffles Grand Hotel d'Angkor** (tel. 063/963888, www.raffles.com/en_ra/property/rga, US$300–2,000), situated just north of the beautifully kept Royal Independence Gardens. From the moment you approach the perfectly restored building, the old world ambience is unbeatable. The Grand d'Angkor first opened in 1932, then catering to the upscale French travelers visiting the ruins of Angkor. Later, illustrious celebrities such as Charlie Chaplin and Jackie Kennedy stayed here. Today the hotel still caters to Cambodia's most affluent guests and the large rooms and suites offer all international-standard amenities, always in a tasteful, francophone, colonial context. The swimming pool is one of the largest in town and the Elephant Bar in the basement exudes quiet retro charm. The Grand d'Angkor is a bit formal, but that's part of the ambience. *Apsara* dance show dinners, performed on the hotel stage behind the pool, take place between October and July and cost US$32. Guests may also avail themselves to the hotel's tennis courts. The Café d'Angkor offers international cuisine and breakfast and

the Restaurant Le Grand serves an exclusive selection of the best of Khmer cuisine. The Grand D'Angkor organizes exclusive tours into the surrounding countryside (including a Khmer-style ranch barbecue combined with a horseback ride) and can even provide food and beverage catering for your private jet. Finally, to get rid of your aches and pains, visit the in-house Amrita Spa, which offers massage therapies, body wraps, packs, and masks, as well as specialized skin care treatments, salt rubs, and manicures. You will be pampered.

Bombastic style, dramatic history, overwhelming architecture, cool retro ambience, and an extremely high standard of services make the **Hotel de la Paix** (tel. 063/966000, www.hoteldelapaixangkor.com, US$330–715) one of the most exclusive, smart, and impressive hotel experiences in the region. The original Hotel de la Paix was built in the 1950s and saw much of Cambodia's tragic history unfold within its walls. Built by a Khmer warlord and anti-French guerilla, who was thought to have magical powers, the hotel has served as the private residence of a Lon Nol commander, as a rice depot for the Khmer Rouge, as government guesthouse during the Vietnamese presence, and finally as the Directorate of UNTAC. In 1993, the old building was knocked down and construction started on the massive art deco edifice the hotel has now become. Arranged around a courtyard with an old banyan tree in its center, more than a hundred luxurious, spacious, and carefully designed rooms cater to every whim. The suites have bathtubs right in the center of the master bedroom, a perfect honeymoon indulgence. All rooms feature pre-programmed iPods, a safe, fridge, and complimentary Wi-Fi. The in-house restaurant, Meric, offers first-class Cambodian cuisine as well as international dishes (main courses around US$25). Guests can choose to dine sitting on swinging platforms, or more conventionally, at a table. Last but not least, the spacious and idiosyncratic pool, complete with an ornate bridge crossing it, is fit for a Roman orgy.

FOOD
Street Cafés and Bakeries

Common Grounds (tel. 063/965687, daily 7 A.M.–10 P.M.) is an agreeable, modern American-style coffeehouse behind Phsar Kandal, with a great collection of teas, cakes, and tarts, free Wi-Fi, and fast Internet terminals. All profits go to NGO projects in Cambodia.

Right next to the French Cultural Center just off Wat Bo Road, **Le Café** (tel. 092/271392, daily 7:30 A.M.–10 P.M.) is located in a quiet garden and offers sandwiches, salads, cakes, and fruit juices, all prepared by the Paul Dubrule Hotel and Tourism School, an NGO training young Cambodians in the hotel and catering business.

The laid-back **Singing Tree Café** (tel. 092/635500, www.singingtreecafe.com) is located in a wooden house in a pretty garden on the eastern side of the river, not more than a few minutes' walk from the Old Market. The food is mostly vegetarian, but also includes sushi. The café is part of the NGO scene in Siem Reap and several worthy causes are promoted here. Movies, often interesting documentaries, are shown in the upstairs lounge area every Thursday at 7 P.M. There are Pilates lessons on Tuesdays, Wednesdays, and Fridays; meditation on Wednesdays; and a monk chat—a chance to interact with and ask questions of Buddhist monks—every Saturday. Check the website for exact times. A small shop sells locally made souvenirs and T-shirts, and the coffee's not bad, either.

Khmer

Several cheap Khmer restaurants can be found tucked to the northeastern side of the Old Market. They all serve good-quality local dishes, most around US$2. Lots of Khmer eat here, which is as good a recommendation as any. All these eateries have English menus with photos. The best of the lot might be **Socheata,** which does an excellent fish *amok* for US$3. Don't be intimidated by the no-thrills decor, since this might be your best chance to taste genuine Khmer cuisine if you are only visiting

Seam Reap. Young Cambodians are trained to work in the restaurant business at the nonprofit "School of Rice" **Sala Bai** (tel. 063/963329, www.salabai.com), a small eatery on Taphul Road, which only opens during term time, from October to July. The restaurant is open on weekdays for lunch only between noon–2 P.M. The students serve quality Asian and Western three-course set menus.

Located on the first-floor terrace of a traditional wooden house on Oum Khun Street to the west of Taphul Road, the **Tany Khmer Family Kitchen** (tel. 063/964118, daily lunch and dinner) offers moderately priced (most courses around US$4) Cambodian dishes, as well as a Khmer Set Menu (US$11). Great home cooking and informal atmosphere make this a very unpretentious, relaxing choice.

The attractive **Sugar Palm Restaurant** (tel. 063/964838, daily 11 A.M.–10 P.M.) on Taphul Road is located on the first floor of a wooden house, a nicely furnished open balcony space, and serves superior Khmer cuisine. Grilled eggplant with minced pork (US$5) and, for the more courageous, frog legs in ginger (US$6) are typical dishes and the wine list is extensive. Diners can also enjoy Cambodia's national dish here: *prahoc* (fermented fish-paste).

The **Khmer Family Restaurant** (tel. 015/999909, daily 11 A.M.–10 P.M.) is part of a colonial block reaching all the way from The Passage, a narrow alley of galleries and restaurants, to the road west of the Old Market. It serves cheap Khmer dishes in a relaxed atmosphere. Try fried morning glory with chicken, pork, beef, fish, or tofu for US$2.50, or fried pumpkin with a choice of the same add-ons for US$3.

Also located in The Passage, the tiny and comfortable **Chamkar Vegetarian Restaurant** (Mon.–Sat. 11 A.M.–10 P.M.) offers a small but very attractive menu of vegetarian Khmer dishes, along with some great cakes.

An altogether different dining experience in the Old Market area is the ultra-trendy **AHA** (tel. 063/965501), founded by the owner of the Hotel de la Paix. Enjoy fine wines and Cambodian and Western snack food and marvel at the contemporary interior design, more than a million miles from the rice fields of Cambodia, and yet somehow sitting (metaphorically speaking) right amongst them. Start with tapas and move on to chicken spring rolls. The restaurant is linked to the McDermott Photo Gallery, creating an artistic, up-market ambience unrivalled in Siem Reap.

On the southern half of Wat Bo Road, the upscale **Viroth's Restaurant** (tel. 012/826346, daily 11 A.M.–2 P.M. for lunch and 6–10:30 P.M. for dinner) has great ambience, with soft lighting and Cambodian tapestries providing a romantic backdrop to the excellent Khmer cuisine. Fish and beef *amok* are favorites. Main dishes cost around US$7.

Facing the west side of the Old Market, the **Champey Restaurant** and the **Amok Restaurant** almost flow into each other across a narrow alley. The former has yellow decor, the latter is kept all in blue; both eateries share the same owner and menus of great Khmer cuisine, and are open daily 9 A.M.–11 P.M. Main courses are around US$5.

Asian

For those who'd like to try health-conscious Asian cuisine, the **Panida Restaurant** (tel. 011/741628, daily 7 A.M.–10 P.M.) offers a decent variety of vegetarian Thai food, guaranteed free of MSG, along with fruit shakes and coffees. Most dishes are around US$4. It's located on the way to the airport, but still close enough to the downtown area to walk there.

The excellent **Chivit Thai** (tel. 012/830761, daily 7 A.M.–10 P.M.) is located in a wooden pavilion fronting a small garden on Wat Bo Road and serves a wide variety of authentic Thai cuisine. Try the *nam prik pla pon,* a fiery fish paste dip served with raw and cooked vegetables, or for a more conventional taste, the excellent chicken cashew. Most dishes are a very reasonable US$4, the food is nicely presented, and the service is prompt. If only they did not play airport lounge music all day…

Right next door, the **Chiang Mai Thai Food** (tel. 012/980833, daily 7 A.M.–midnight) is

equally authentic and reliable, but is located in an air-conditioned building. The food here is slightly cheaper than at the Chivit Thai, but it tastes just as good and there's a large variety of dishes to choose from.

The **Sawasdee Food Garden** (tel. 063/964456, www.yaklom.com, daily 6:30 A.M.–10 P.M.) on Wat Bo Road, just north of Route 6, serves decent Thai food in a laid-back atmosphere. *Tom yum kung,* shrimp soup, as spicy as you order it, is US$5.

The **Paris-Saigon** (tel. 063/965408, daily 11 A.M.–10 P.M.) is a cozy restaurant in the Wat Bo area, with attractive red-brick decor. The menu is predominantly French, but there are a few Vietnamese courses as well, and a good selection of wines. Try the beef fillet (US$9.50) and *phoe bho beef* (Vietnamese beef soup, US$6). It's a great place for a quiet dinner for two.

Located in a family house and decorated with Japanese paintings, the **Maido Yakiniku BBQ Restaurant** (tel. 063/761947, daily lunch and dinner), on a road parallel and west of Taphul Road, is as low-key a Japanese restaurant as you could hope for, with common and private VIP rooms (for groups of up to six). Dishes include sushi as well as some Khmer dishes, such as grill-it-yourself barbecues of beef imported from Australia.

The **Hong Kong Restaurant** (tel. 063/966226, daily 9 A.M.–10 P.M.), to the north of the Old Market and just south of Center Market, is a small, bright, fast-food-style Chinese eatery, offering dim sum and a wide range of standard Chinese rice dishes.

The **d'Wau Restaurant** (tel. 012/356030, daily 7 A.M.–10 P.M.), on Wat Bo Road, is a smart and trendy-looking Malaysian restaurant with an extensive menu of curries. Guests can dine in tiny wooden pavilions in a small garden out front or in the large air-conditioned restaurant. Try the chicken satay (US$3). The d'Wau is 100 percent halal and does not sell alcohol. It's possible to have food delivered to your hotel.

Little India (tel. 012/652398, daily 9 A.M.–late), located right in the heart of the Old

Market area, is actually a Sri Lankan place, but serves reliable Indian cooking. *Thalis* are US$3–4, depending on whether you prefer vegetables or meat, and you can sit right on the curbside to watch the nightlife action.

The cheap and cheerful **Maharaja** (tel. 063/966221) manages to conjure magic at a small price in the heart of the Old Market area. Vegetarian *thalis* cost just US$2.50 and they are not bad. Guests may choose from five different levels of spiciness. All the usual Indian and Pakistani standards are available, from trusty chicken tikka to creamy *korma* dishes, with most main courses around US$4. Service is prompt and friendly.

The **East India Curry Restaurant** (tel. 063/966898) on the sixth floor of the Claremont Angkor Hotel serves a huge choice of Indian and South Asian dishes. Meat standards such as chicken tikka are around US$6, while vegetarian courses will set you back around US$4. The East India has two terraces, both offering good views over Siem Reap.

Possibly the tastiest Indian restaurant is **Curry Walla** (tel. 063/965451), a Punjabi place on Sibvatha Boulevard that does very good *dal makhni*. Most dishes, both vegetarian and non-vegetarian, are around US$3.

International

North of the Old Market and almost next door to the Hong Kong Restaurant, the **Happy Herb Pizza** (daily 7 A.M.–11 P.M.) serves budget Khmer dishes and pizzas, as "happy"—meaning topped with marijuana—as you like 'em. It's part of a franchise with outlets in Phnom Penh.

Tell Siem Reap (tel. 063/963289, daily 11 A.M.–10 P.M.) on Sivatha Boulevard, like its namesake in Phnom Penh, offers a large variety of German and Asian dishes from around US$7 in an air-conditioned, family-friendly environment; there's a good choice of German beers and liquors.

The **X Rooftop Bar** (daily 4 P.M.–sunrise) on Sivatha Boulevard is one of the most popular after-dark hangouts in Siem Reap. Movies, free Wi-Fi, Western comfort food, cigars, wine,

and a great view make this a great stopover on any tour through the town's nightlife area.

One of the best-restored, spectacular-looking, colonial-style restaurants is **Le Malraux** (tel. 063/966041, www.le-malraux-siem-reap. com), located on Sivatha Boulevard opposite the road that leads to the Angkor Night Market. A modern art-deco dream, with a menu and wine list to suit the ambience, Le Malraux is the kind of place you might head (scrubbed and showered, of course) after a dusty day amongst the Angkor ruins, to enjoy a cigar and a cognac and debate the legacy of the French Republic in the Kingdom of Cambodia. Main dishes are around US$12.

The **Abacus** (tel. 012/644286, daily 10 A.M.–11 P.M.), just off Taphul Street, is an agreeable French and Khmer restaurant in a traditional Cambodian house located in a small garden. It sports a short but interesting menu. The eatery feels almost like the living room of an absent-minded academic, with books and magazines piled on shelves everywhere and small tables separated by low walls inviting guests to linger over food and wines. Dishes include fish fillet tamarind (US$7.50), mashed pumpkin, and grilled eggplant; the crocodile tail curry (US$13) is highly recommended for more adventurous diners.

Le Jardin des Délices, an excellent restaurant that is part of the Paul Dubrule Hotel and Tourism School (tel. 063/963672, www.ecolep-auldubrule.org), way out on the road to the airport, opens only from October to July, during the school's term time. Set lunches prepared by the students are US$11. Call ahead.

On the corner of Corner Oum Khun Street and Street 14, in the Wat Bo area, **L'Escale des Arts & des Sens** (tel. 063/761442) serves upscale French cuisine in a large comfortable pavilion. Grilled duck foie gras with lemongrass, ginger juice, and talamma seed is US$24. Set menus are between US$18–24. Occasional dance and music performances are put on in high season.

Viva (tel. 092/209154, daily 11:30 A.M.–late) is Siem Reap's only Mexican restaurant. Located on a corner to the northern side of the Old

Market, this is obviously the place to go if you have a craving for burritos and enchiladas and want to watch the world go by from street level. Expect to pay about US$5 a main course.

Located in a whitewashed colonial building near Wat Damnak, the stylish **Alliance Café** (tel. 063/964940, daily 10 A.M.–midnight) is a smart French restaurant run by a French chef, made especially attractive by the works of Cambodian and French artists. Usually two or three artists exhibit their work at any given time. There's also outdoor seating. Red tuna coated with sesame (US$16) is recommended. Several Khmer dishes are also on offer.

The **Red Pizza Shop** (daily 10 A.M.–10 P.M.), near Kandal Market, smacks of a well-known American franchise, but offers pizzas unheard of in the United States. Try Pizza Tom Yum and other combinations catering to Asian tastes, as well as more conventional cheese and meat toppings.

Pissa Italiana (daily 11 A.M.–11 P.M., except closed Sun. lunch) on Pub Street is a reliable Italian eatery, serving pastas, pizzas, salads, and delicious homemade lemon tarts.

The **Jasmine Angkor** (tel. 012/808881, 24 hours a day) on Samdech Tep Vong Street near the corner of Taphul Road, is not particularly cozy, but it does offer air-conditioning and a huge menu of Khmer and European dishes (main courses around US$4). Traditional dance performances take place occasionally in the evenings.

One of the trendiest and most cosmopolitan places in town is the futuristic **Blue Pumpkin** (tel. 063/963574), on the road north of the Old Market. It offers not just a comfortable, air-conditioned, first-floor lounge with Wi-Fi access, but also has some of Siem Reap's best sandwiches, salads, cakes, and tarts on its menu. It's no wonder this place is enormously popular with the backpacker set.

INFORMATION AND SERVICES
Tourist Information

The Tourist Office, next to Le Grand d'Angkor Hotel, is not terribly informed and most visitors cull their information from local guides, hotels and guesthouses, and the ever-present free Canby guides, which list hotels and restaurants. Cambodia Pocket Guides publish a couple of booklets featuring shopping, dining, and drinking. These publications promote only businesses that advertise.

Libraries and Permanent Exhibitions
THE CENTRE OF KHMER STUDIES AT WAT DAMNAK

This excellent non-lending library (tel. 063/96438, www.khmerstudies.org/library/library.htm), located on the eastern side of the river within the Wat Damnak temple compound, is open to the public Monday–Saturday 8 A.M.–noon and 2–5 P.M. The Centre of Khmer Studies promotes research, teaching, and public service in the social sciences, arts, and humanities. The library holds a large collection of books and academic texts in English, French, Khmer, and several other languages. It's possible to have texts photocopied.

THE TONLÉ SAP EXHIBITION

Out on the road to the temples, the NGO Krousar Thmey, a foundation helping deprived children, has set up a small exhibition on Khmer heritage and the ecology of the Tonlé Sap Lake. The exhibits (daily 8 A.M.–noon and 1:30–5:30 P.M.) look a bit dated, but a relaxing massage by blind masseurs trained by physiotherapists (US$5/hour) is also available here. You can just drop by or call ahead for an appointment (tel. 063/964694).

Money

Siem Reap is dotted with banks and ATMs and there are unofficial money changers at Phsar Kandal (Center Market) that offer a marginally better rate than the banks. Banks are usually open Monday–Friday 8 A.M.–3 or 4 P.M., and sometimes until 11:30 A.M. on Saturdays.

All ATMs, including those at the airport, dispense U.S. dollars. Large ripped dollar notes will not be accepted by local businesses.

Credit cards (especially Visa, MasterCard, and JCB) are widely accepted, but businesses usually charge a commission (of a few percent) for transactions. Travelers checks are accepted at most banks, at some hotels, and by some money changers.

Health and Emergencies

In case of a serious accident or illness, head for the 24-hour **Royal Angkor International Hospital** (tel. 063/761888, 012/235888, 063/399111, www.royalangkorhospital.com) on the road to the airport, which provides high-quality medical services (including an ICU and blood bank), as well as an all-Cambodia ambulance service. The hospital can also organize medical evacuations in very serious situations.

The most recommended pharmacies are U-Care in the Old Market area (tel. 063/965396) and at the airport. Make sure you have medical insurance (highly recommended in Cambodia), as hospital bills can be astronomical.

Internet Access

Siem Reap is extremely well-connected to the digital global village. In fact, virtually every guesthouse and hotel provides Internet access to its guests, either on communal terminals or with Wi-Fi access in the rooms. Sometimes, especially in mid-range places, this service is free of charge; at other establishments, you might have to buy a card or charge the time spent online to your bill. Some bars and restaurants, including the Blue Pumpkin, Common Grounds, and the X Bar, have free Wi-Fi access, and there are plenty of Internet cafés around town from where Skype calls are usually possible. Rates average US$1 per hour.

Post Office

The post office, located on the western side of the river, a little south of the FCC, is open daily 7:30 A.M.–5:30 P.M. and there's no vouching as to how reliable it is. If you're shipping something valuable, then DHL (Phsar Kandal, tel. 063/964949) might be the ticket.

Laundry

Virtually all hotels, from budget flophouses to first-class boutique hotels, offer a laundry service.

GETTING THERE
Air

Most of the two million international travelers who visit the Angkor ruins each year arrive at Siem Reap's modern airport. As Bangkok Airways/Siem Reap Airways have a monopoly on flights from Thailand, prices on this route, the busiest, are unreasonably high; it's actually cheaper to fly into Phnom Penh with Air Asia and then on to Siem Reap on a domestic flight with Siem Reap Airways, though this of course is a lot of hassle. Still, while the road between the Thai border and Siem Reap is still unfinished, Bangkok Airways is the most convenient choice, with five direct Bangkok–Siem Reap flights a day. This monopoly may end upon completion of the highway.

It's also possible to fly into Siem Reap from Singapore on Silk Air, from Kuala Lumpur on Malaysia Airlines and Air Asia, from Ho Chi Minh City and Hanoi on Vietnam Airlines, from Kunming in China on China Eastern Airlines, from Cheng Du on Angkor Airways, from Inchon in South Korea on Korean Air and Asiana Airlines, and from Hong Kong with Dragon Air and Siem Reap Airways.

The airport is six kilometers from town; a taxi costs US$5, and a *motodup* will take you for US$1. Note that the domestic departure tax is US$6, while the international departure tax is US$25. Many hotels provide free pick-ups and drop-offs, if you make arrangements in advance.

AIRLINE OFFICES

Siem Reap has the following airline offices:

- **Angkor Airways:** 564, Mondul Village, tel. 063/964878, www.angkorairways.com

- **Bangkok Airways/Siem Reap Airways:** National Route No. 6, tel. 063/965442, www.bangkokair.com

- **China Eastern Airlines:** 304, Steung Thmey Village, Svay Dangkum Commune, tel. 063/965229, www.ce-air.com
- **Korean Air:** Room 120, Airlines Office Building, Siem Reap International Airport, tel. 063/964881, www.koreanair.com
- **Lao Airlines:** 114, Sala Khanseng Village, National Route No. 6, tel. 063/963283, www.laoairlines.com
- **Malaysia Airlines:** Rooms 117–119, Siem Reap International Airport, tel. 063/964761, www.malaysiaairlines.com.my
- **Silk Air:** Room 122–123, Airline Office Building, Siem Reap International Airport, tel. 063/964993
- **Vietnam Airlines:** 342, National Route No. 6, tel. 063/964488, www.vietnamairlines.com

Boat

The boat rides from Phnom Penh and Battambang are enjoyable in the wet and cool season, but several accidents have happened in the past, with vessels breaking down mid-lake (or running out of gas) and luggage being lost. What with road conditions getting better all the time and passenger numbers on the ferry dropping off, the boat operators have raised the prices. Still, if you are itching for a bit of adventure, try the run to Phnom Penh for US$30, or to Battambang for US$20. The four- to six-hour ferry ride to Phnom Penh is only moderately scenic, but the trip to Battambang (6–8 hours) definitely has its moments, as the boat passes several traditional fishing villages on stilts before entering the Sangker River, which snakes through numerous small settlements before reaching Cambodia's second city.

These ferries are not altogether safe by Western standards, and the buses are considerably cheaper and faster.

Regional Road Transport

Numerous bus companies do the Phnom Penh to Siem Reap run, which costs US$8–11, depending on the on-board facilities (all buses on this route are air-conditioned). Buses by Sorya Transport (tel. 023/210359), Mekong Express (tel. 063/963662), which has deluxe, air-conditioned buses, Paramount Angkor (tel. 063/761912), and Capitol Guesthouse (tel. 023/217627) all leave from the Chong Kov Sou Bus Station, off Route 6, a couple of kilometers to the west of Siem Reap. *Motodups* will take you there for US$2, tuk-tuks for US$3. Journey times are typically 5–6 hours and buses leave very frequently 7 A.M.–14:30 P.M. Most guesthouses and hotels are happy to get the tickets for you, but may charge an extra dollar for the service.

With rising gas prices and affluent tourists, taxi fares from Siem Reap have risen to almost extortionate heights. A private taxi to Phnom Penh is pricy at US$75, while a ride to Battambang is US$50. A ride to the border town of Poipet will set you back about US$60. Coming from Phnom Penh or Battambang might be cheaper. Coming from the border, you will have to deal with the Poipet taxi mafia who might demand anything from US$40 to US$70. The price will partly depend on your bargaining skills.

The Siem Reap-Bangkok Run

It's possible to travel from Siem Reap to Bangkok overland in one long day. Numerous operators offer the trip, which takes around 9–12 hours. Ask your guesthouse or hotel for details. From Bangkok, a number of operators on Khao San Road offer the trip for US$10–20, but this is fraught with scams and rip-offs. Sometimes passengers are taken through the Pailin border, at other times, the buses on the Cambodian side are so slow that travelers arrive late and tired in Siem Reap, more likely than not to accept the choice of accommodation offered by the bus touts, who collect commission. Going it alone from Siem Reap need not be more expensive, as there is now a bus for US$10 to the border in Poipet. Alternatively, you can take a taxi (US$50–70, 3–4 hours). On the Thai side, you can choose between bus (150–200 baht), minibus (300–400 baht), or train (50 baht) all the way to the Thai capital—or, if you arrive late, to a decent hotel or guesthouse in Aranyaprathet, the town closest to the border on the Thai side. Avoid staying overnight in Poipet at all costs.

GETTING AROUND

Downtown Siem Reap is small enough to walk around, but if you are staying a bit farther out, there's a range of local transport you can use to get around town. Besides hiring a bicycle from a guesthouse for a couple of dollars a day, the cheapest options are the trusty *motodups*,

motorcycle taxis that will charge about 1,000 riel for a short ride, up to US$1 for a longer distance. Prices increase as soon as the sun's gone down. A tuk-tuk is a safer, more comfortable, and slightly more expensive option—with rides in town for around 2,000 riel to US$1. Unless you are going to the airport (US$5), a taxi around town seems hardly worth it.

Foreigners are not allowed to drive themselves in the Siem Reap area, unless they are residents. This guarantees income to the *motodups* and tuk-tuk drivers who depend on tourist dollars.

Angkor

Most visitors to Cambodia come to see the temples of Angkor. Located in forests to the northwest of the Tonlé Sap Lake, the sprawling ruins of the Angkor Empire are simply without equal in Southeast Asia. It is the interplay between forest and ruins that gives the former Khmer capital its otherworldly, fantastical atmosphere. Even widely traveled and jaded culture-hounds cannot help but be moved by the scale and sensuousness of these buildings.

More than two million visitors entered the Angkor Archaeological Park in 2008. For Cambodians, Angkor lies at the heart of the national identity: as much an ancient success story and an object of immense pride as a psychological burden for a country with such a tragic recent history.

For more than 500 years, Angkor dominated the political and cultural affairs of much of Southeast Asia and the Khmer Empire spread into large parts of Thailand, as well as Laos and Vietnam—restored temples in Thailand and Laos attest to this—before being subsumed by its own grandeur and the jungle in the 15th century.

Angkor Wat is the largest religious building in the world, and its surroundings play host to the highest concentration of temples in the world. The temples were declared a UNESCO World Heritage site in 1992. Around the

© AROON THAEWCHATTURAT

the central pyramid of Angkor Wat

temples, life goes on as it has done for hundreds of years. Siem Reap Province is one of the poorest in Cambodia and rice-fields continue to be tilled by oxen and plow, just as they were during the Khmer Empire's hey-day. In fact, many aspects of Cambodian life have not changed much in the past thousand years. Since the fall of Angkor in 1431 at the hands of the Siamese, the country has been sliding from one tragedy into another, and many Cambodians dream of recapturing some of the country's former glory one day.

What is considered Angkor today (part of the Angkor Archaeological Park) spreads over an area of some 230 square kilometers, and besides Angkor Wat and the imperial city of Angkor Thom, this includes all other temples in the region. Most temples lie a few kilometers to the north of Siem Reap, while the structures known as the Roluos Group, which predates Angkor slightly, can be found 15 kilometers east of Siem Reap.

THE HISTORY OF THE ANGKOR EMPIRE

The wall of the city is some five miles in circumference. It has five gates, each with double portals. Two gates pierce the eastern side; the other sides have one gate only. Outside the wall stretches a great moat, across which access to the city is given by massive causeways. Flanking the causeways on each side are fifty-four divinities resembling warlords in stone, huge and terrifying. All five gates are similar. The parapets of the causeways are of solid stone, carved to represent nine-headed serpents. The fifty-four divinities grasp the serpents with their hands, seemingly to prevent their escape. Above each gate are grouped five gigantic heads of Buddha, four of them facing the four cardinal points of the compass, the fifth, brilliant with gold, holds a central position.

This is how Chou Ta-Kuan, a Chinese diplomat described the Khmer capital of Angkor Thom during his visit in the late 13th century in his account *The Customs of Cambodia* (The Siam Society, Bangkok, 1992). The visitor from the North was clearly impressed by the power and affluence projected by the city's monuments, which, at the time, were the culmination of 500

years of the rise and fall of one of the greatest empires of the Middle Ages. To put the glory of Angkor in perspective: When Chou Ta-Kuan visited, the imperial city of Angkor Thom had around one million inhabitants, and the temple of Ta Prohm alone had more than 80,000 servants and staff, while in Europe, Paris had a population of just 25,000.

The history of Angkor begins some 500 years prior to Chou Ta-Kuan's visit, at the dawn of the 9th century. In the preceding centuries, smaller empires and fiefdoms had fallen and risen in the region, which we now recognize as Cambodia. Most of them had fallen under the control of the court of Java in Indonesia, although some recent studies suggest that Java could in fact be Chenla, an earlier Khmer kingdom. Whatever the case, the first great Khmer king Jayavarman II (A.D. 802–850) declared himself *devaraja* (divine ruler) of the kingdom of Kambujadesa; he established several capitals, including one at Phnom Kulen, to the northeast of Siem Reap, and later another at Hariharalaya, near Roluos.

Towards the end of the 9th century, Indravarman I (A.D. 877–889) built the first of the great Angkor temples, Preah Ko, as well as the Bakong and began work on a huge *baray* (water reservoir), at Hariharalaya. His son, Yasovarman I (A.D. 889–900) expanded on his father's achievements, finished the *baray,* and created yet another royal city, Yashodarapura, located around Phnom Bakheng, today's most popular sunset spot within the Angkor Archaeological Park. Yasovarman I might also have been the Khmer king to begin construction of the mountain temple of Preah Vihear. Other kings came and went, powers struggles between different royal families and with the neighboring Cham continued, and the capital briefly moved out to Koh Ker, before returning to the Angkor area.

Suryavarman II, who ascended to the throne in A.D. 1113, extended the Khmer Empire to its largest territory. He also built Angkor Wat, yet following his death in A.D. 1150, the empire fell apart once more. Only his cousin, Jayavarman VII, managed to reunite the kingdom under

CHOU TA-KUAN: ANGKOR'S CHRONICLER

Chou Ta-Kuan, a Chinese diplomat in the service of Emperor Chengzong of Yaun, grandson of Kublai Khan, traveled from Wenzhou, on the East China Sea coast, past Guangzhou and Hainan, along Vietnam's coast and up the Mekong River as far as Kompong Cham, from where he took a smaller vessel across the Tonlé Sap Lake to arrive at the imperial city of Angkor Thom in August 1296.

Chou Ta-Kuan was neither the first nor the last Chinese diplomat to visit the seat of the Angkor Empire, but he stayed for 11 months and took notes. *The Customs of*

Cambodia, the only surviving first-person account of life in the Khmer Empire, is one of the most important sources available to scholars and laymen to understand Angkor. Not only did the diplomat describe the city of Angkor Thom, he also shed some light on the daily lives of ordinary Cambodians. With his report, Chou Ta-Kuan gives today's visitors an opportunity to imagine how the ruined splendor of the temples must once have been a busy metropolis and how, at its height, a million people could have lived and worked here.

his crown in A.D. 1181, fight off the Cham, and commence the Khmer Empire's last great renaissance. Jayavarman VII converted from Hinduism to Mahayana Buddhism, founded the last great Khmer city, Angkor Thom, and oversaw Angkor's most prolific period of monument building. In less than 40 years, hundreds of temples—as well as libraries, *dharamshalas* (rest houses), and hospitals—were hastily constructed along new roads that now connected large parts of the kingdom. Many of the monuments built under Jayavarman VII are artistically inferior and stylistically impure because the speed of construction was so frenetic. It seemed like the last god-king knew that time was running out. It was Jayavarman VII who had some of Angkor's most enduring iconic buildings constructed, including Ta Prohm and the Bayon. In A.D. 1203, the king annexed Champa and effectively extended his empire to southern Vietnam. But, with the death of Jayavarman VII in A.D. 1218, the moment had passed and Angkor slowly went into decline.

Hinduism was briefly reintroduced by Jayavarman VIII in the late 13th century, resulting in a concerted and presumably costly act of vandalism that saw the defacing of many Buddhist monuments, including Ta Prohm and Preah Khan. Buddhism soon returned, but in a different form, as Theravada Buddhism, which has survived in Cambodia

to this day and which puts less emphasis on the divinity of the king. Perhaps this loss of spiritual authority affected later kings. Perhaps, as new research suggests, the Angkor Empire had overreached itself, ruined the environment around Siem Reap, and was ready to give way to something else.

Repeated incursions by the Siamese culminated in a seven-month siege of Angkor Thom in A.D. 1431, after which King Ponhea Yat moved the capital southwest to Phnom Penh. Other reasons for the demise of this great empire are also plausible. The Khmer Empire had been built on the back of an agrarian society and trade was becoming more important in Southeast Asia. Angkor Thom was too isolated, too far from the coast, and too far from the Mekong to be able to keep up with new challenges. Following the move to Phnom Penh, the temples remained active, yet were slowly subsumed by jungle.

THE "REDISCOVERY" OF ANGKOR

Angkor is unlikely to have ever been completely abandoned, though exact information on the activities around the ruins between the 15th and 18th century A.D. is sketchy. Following the last onslaught by the Thais in 1431 and the gradual shift of the capital towards Phnom Penh, monks continued to live around Angkor

Wat until the 16th century. The Cambodian court apparently returned to Angkor for brief periods during the 16th and 17th centuries.

Around the same time, an early report by the Portuguese writer Diego De Couto apparently referred to a Capuchin friar visiting the region in 1585 and finding the temples in ruins, overgrown by vegetation. So impressed were early visitors from Europe, the Middle East, and other parts of Asia that some wildly speculated that the Romans or Alexander the Great had built the temples.

A trickle of these adventurers and traders, many of whom had settled at the court in Phnom Penh in the 16th century, began to take note of the ruins, either by hearing other people's accounts or traveling there themselves, a 10-day journey at the time. A group of Spanish missionaries even hoped to rehabilitate the ruins and turn them into a center of Christian teaching. A Japanese interpreter, Kenryo Shimano, drew the first accurate ground plan of Angkor Wat in the early 17th century. Japanese writing on a pillar inside Angkor Wat is said to have been carved by his son, who later visited the site in honor of his adventurous father. Other foreigners—including an American, a Brit, and several French explorers—published their accounts of visiting the temples, but no one really took note.

In 1858, Henri Mouhot, a French naturalist who lived on the island of Jersey, set off on an expedition sponsored by the British Royal Geographical Society and reached Angkor in early 1860. Mouhot spent three weeks at Angkor, surveyed the temples, and continued up the Mekong into Laos, where he eventually died of a fever (possibly malaria). His notes were published in 1864, a year after Cambodia had become a French protectorate.

THE RESTORATION OF ANGKOR

In 1863, a year before Mouhot's report was published, Vice-Admiral Bonard, the governor of the French colony of Cochin China (South Vietnam), visited Angkor and decided that it had not been the Romans or any other foreign power who had built the magnificent temples, but the now-impoverished Cambodians.

The idea of restoring Cambodia and its people to its former grandeur encouraged the population back home in France to support the republic's quickly expanding and unpopular colonial efforts in Southeast Asia. Angkor became a symbol of this drive, and as a consequence, was soon very much a focus of attention at the highest political levels of the French administration. Thailand was already under the influence of the British (a British photographer, John Thomson, published the first images of Angkor Wat in the 1860s), and the race was on to find a trade route into China, which was just beginning to open up to foreign commerce. Cambodia and the Mekong were to play a key role in this race.

In 1866, the Mekong Exploration Commission, led by Doudart de Lagrée, France's representative in Cambodia, and accompanied by Francis Garnier, Louis Delaporte, a photographer named Gsell, and several others, set off to find out whether the Mekong was navigable. On the way, they made a planned detour to Angkor and took detailed, scientific notes. Louis Delaporte's watercolors and drawings, fanciful though they were, and Gsell's photographs of the temples, along with route maps and extensive descriptions of temples and the lives of Cambodians, were published in two volumes in 1873 as *Voyage d'exploration en Indo-Chine*. As the French public was not aware of Henri Mouhot's British-funded efforts, Garnier and Delaporte (de Lagré had died by this time) got all the credit for the "discovery" of Angkor. Their findings were well presented and included, for the first time, outlying temples such as Beng Melea, Preah Khan, and Wat Nokor, to the east of Angkor, as well as Khmer temples in southern Laos. Of course, in the eyes of superior-minded Europeans, the temples could not compete in grandeur with efforts back home and the early explorers claimed that "Cambodian art ought to perhaps rank its productions behind the greatest masterpieces in the West."

Yet, slowly, in the minds of these early

archaeologists and consequently the French public, the true dimensions of the Khmer Empire began to emerge. In 1867, at the Universal Exposition in Paris, visitors were presented with giant plaster cast reproductions of the temples. In the following years, Delaporte returned to Cambodia and began to systematically remove statues, sculptures, and stonework to Europe. Soon after, he became the director of the Indochinese Museum in Paris, which began to amass a collection of Angkorian artifacts. Around the same time, the first tourists began to arrive. They too took souvenirs with them, many of which disappeared into private homes in France. In 1887, the French architect Lucien Fournereau made extensive and detailed drawings of Angkor Wat and other temples, which for the first time, presented Europeans with accurate, scientific plans of Khmer architecture. Hendrick Kern, a Dutchman, managed to decipher the Sanskrit inscriptions on temple walls in 1879, and the French epigrapher Etienne Aymonier undertook a first inventory of the temples around Angkor, listing 910 monuments in all.

In 1898, the Ecole Francaise d'Extreme Orient (EFEO), founded by the colonial masters to study various aspects of their Far-Eastern possessions, began to work in Cambodia, and soon efforts were made to start clearing the jungle from some of the ruins. The EFEO created a road network around the ruins, the Petit Circuit and the Grand Circuit, which are still used by many visitors. To this day, the EFEO has been the most consistent body involved in the study and restoration of Angkor.

The Cambodians were never consulted about any of France's activities around Angkor. The French writer Pierre Loti remarked in 1912 that France "was idiotically desperate to rule over Asia, which has existed since time immemorial, and to disrupt the course of things there." Loti felt that the French presence was disrupting the continuity of Cambodia, where the royal dancers appeared to step out of the past into the present, unchanged by time. The writer stated: "Times we thought were forever past are revived here before our eyes; nothing

has changed here, either in the spirit of the people or in the heart of their palaces." The French artist Auguste Rodin was so taken with the dancers that he followed them around France on their visit in 1906.

At the time, Angkor, which lay in Siem Reap Province, still belonged to Siam. It was only in 1907 that France forced Siam to hand over three provinces under Siamese control, including Siem Reap. From then on, France, the colonial masters of Indochine, were in control of the temples—until the beginning of World War II, when the area briefly returned to Siamese territory, because Siam had aligned herself with the Japanese, who had wrested control of the colonies from the French (although it was officers from the collaborating Vichy France government that continued to administer the rest of Cambodia).

Following World War II, France regained control of Cambodia and the Angkor temples until independence in 1953. This long-term continuity meant that the EFEO had a total monopoly on the research conducted on Angkor, which enabled the scientists involved to develop a coherent body of work over the years. In 1908, Conservation d'Angkor, the archaeological directorate of the Cambodian government, was established in Siem Reap and became responsible for the maintenance of the ruins. The office's first curator, Jean Commaille, originally a painter who'd arrived with the Foreign Legion, lived in a straw hut by the causeway to Angkor Wat, and wrote the very first guidebook to Angkor before being killed by bandits in 1916.

Commaille's successors further cleared the jungle, and, in 1925, Angkor was officially opened as a park, designed to attract tourists. Soon the first batches of foreign visitors arrived, by car or boat, from Phnom Penh or Bangkok and guided tours on elephant back were conducted around the temples. Many of these early tourists, rich globetrotters for the most part, stole priceless items from amongst the ruins or carved their names into the ancient stones. Little could be done about the thefts, but to search a few posh hotel rooms. Tourism continued to increase, and, in 1936, even Charlie Chaplin did a round of the temples.

In the meantime, research techniques used by the EFEO continued to evolve and became more integrated. Initially, different specialists had worked on different aspects of reconstruction and research; it was only in the late 1920s that several disciplines were combined—with spectacular results. Only now could the Bayon and Banteay Srei be dated properly and Angkor's chronology finally took shape. Influenced by the Archaeological Service of the Dutch East Indies, the EFEO, under curator Henri Marchal, began to undertake complete reconstructions of temples in the 1930s, most notably of Banteay Srei. Following World War II, as Cambodia moved towards independence, the EFEO moved its headquarters to France, and Conservation d'Angkor now ran the largest archaeological dig in the world, the French staff slowly being complemented by (French-educated) students from Phnom Penh. Excavations further afield could now be undertaken, at locations like Sambor Prei Kuk, the pre-Angkorian ruins near Kompong Thom.

In the 1960s, Angkor began to be used as a backdrop for movies, most notably *Lord Jim* and some of King Sihanouk's feature films. The ever-growing popularity of the temples meant that looting increased and many statues had to be removed and replaced with new plaster models.

Soon there were new challenges to the continuing restoration efforts—war was coming. Following Sihanouk's fall from power in 1970, the French staff of the EFEO carried on working on the temples for another two years, when they were forced to leave as the Khmer Rouge were closing in. Local workers continued with their efforts until 1975, when the revolutionary communists forced them into the fields to work or executed them. Angkor was once again abandoned. Through the long years of communist revolution and the subsequent civil war, the temples remained off limits, both to researchers and casual visitors, and the jungle grew back over the monuments. The Khmer Rouge was too superstitious to destroy the temples (though they destroyed virtually every modern temple in the country), but many research documents went up in flames. Luckily, much of the work the EFEO had done since its inception, some 70 years of solid, systematic research, had been copied and taken to Paris.

Following the invasion of Vietnam, work slowly resumed in the 1980s. First, the Archaeological Survey of India sent a team to restore Angkor Wat. The efforts of this enterprise have been widely criticized, but it should be kept in mind how very dangerous a country Cambodia was at the time and that the Indian scientists had little materials and few local experts to work with. At the same time, a Polish scientific delegation engaged in excavations around the Bayon. In 1989, the Royal University of Fine Arts was re-opened in Phnom Penh in order to train a new generation of archaeologists.

In 1991, after 20 years of neglect and devastation, not just of the ruins of Angkor, but of Cambodia as a whole, UNESCO (United Nations Educational, Scientific and Cultural Organization) established an office in Cambodia. Soon after, the World Monuments Fund was the first NGO to establish a branch at Angkor, followed shortly after by the return of EFEO. France and Japan soon pledged large funds for safeguarding the ruins, which by now were once more being looted at a frightening rate. Throughout the 1990s, new information garnered from technologies not available prior to 1972, including aerial photographs, and even space radar imagery obtained from NASA's space shuttle Endeavour, began to be systematically assimilated into the larger research body.

In 1992, Angkor Wat, along with 400 other monuments in the area, was included in the UNESCO World Heritage List. This officially made Angkor one of the world's most important cultural sites, a move designed to protect the remnants of the Khmer Empire from further looting or indiscriminate development.

Cambodia now has an article in its constitution that calls on the state to preserve the country's ancient monuments. UNESCO is the international coordinator for international contributions towards the up-keep of the temples. While restoration efforts have continued, and while UNESCO has been pushing for sustainable development, the Cambodian government created APSARA (Authority for the Protection and Management of Angkor and the Region of Siem Reap), a nongovernmental organization in charge of research, protection and conservation of cultural heritage, as well as urban and tourist development, in 1995.

THE FUTURE OF ANGKOR

In the Angkor Archaeological Park, it's the sheer numbers of visitors that now pose the gravest threat to the ruins. Wooden walkways, such as at Ta Prohm and Beng Melea, reduce some of the damage caused by large number of visitors, but with current visitor figures at two million a year, questions of sustainability continue to arise. For this reason, APSARA has been a mixed blessing. Placed under the double supervision of the Presidency of the Council of Ministers (technical supervision) and the Ministry of Economy and Finance (financial supervision), the organization's responsibilities are split into two distinct and sometimes contradictory areas—protection and exploitation. In 1999, the Cambodian government awarded a 10-year lease to manage the income generated by the temples to a private company called Sokimex. Attempts by UNESCO to stem the worst commercial exploits, such as elevator and footwear projects that followed, have had some success.

But Siem Reap's urban infrastructure has not been able to keep pace with tourist development, leading to a breakdown in water distribution and a lack of drainage. This is turn is affecting the temples, which are slowly subsiding, along with the falling water table. The Bayon is sinking into the sandy ground and cracks widen between its carefully assembled stones. In high season, some 6,000 visitors a day clamber across the temples, traffic jams within the park have become commonplace, and the once-romantic sunset spot at Phnom Bakheng is now crowded by a few thousand tourists every evening.

Recent debates about sustainability have centered on diversifying tourism in Cambodia. But even if some of the almost two million or so tourists could be persuaded to look at temples further afield, most first-time visitors to the country will most likely still want to see Angkor. The Cambodian government would like to increase visitor numbers to Angkor to 10 million people a year, five times the current volume.

Incidentally, a French-Australian-Cambodian research project called the Greater Angkor Project indicates that, at its height, Angkor Thom was surrounded by an urban sprawl the size of modern-day Los Angeles and therefore was probably the world's largest pre-industrial urban settlement. According to scientists from Sydney University, the Khmer capital lay in an urbanized wasteland, stripped bare of its forests, its rivers diverted, dependent on a sophisticated irrigation system that proved unsustainable. This, the scientists suggest, was the reason for the collapse of one of the world's great empires. And, according to the Greater Angkor Project, the same mistakes are being made again.

INFORMATION
Entry Tickets and
Hours of Operation

All visitors to the Angkor Archaeological Park must have valid tickets. Visitors are checked at virtually all the temples. If you lose your ticket, there's no replacement and you will have to buy another one.

Tickets are available at the main entrance on the road from Siem Reap to Angkor Wat. One-day (US$20), three-day (US$40), and seven-day (US$60) tickets are available and must be used on consecutive days. One-day tickets are also available at a second entrance off the airport road. Three-day and seven-day tickets need to have a photograph of the ticket holder attached. If you are planning to purchase either of these, it's best to bring your own picture, as queues at the free photography service counter can be long on busy days. The ticket booths on the main road open at 5 A.M. and entry to the temples is possible from 5:30 A.M.–sunset. Banteay Srei closes at 5 P.M., while Kbal Spean closes at 3 P.M. Don't buy tickets anywhere else, as they are likely to be fakes. Note that if you purchase a ticket for the Angkor temples around 5 P.M., it is valid that same evening as well as the next one, three, or seven days. Some visitors use the afternoon prior to their passes becoming valid to visit Phnom Bakheng for the sunset views.

Several of the more remote temples are not covered by the tickets. Entrance to Phnom Kulen costs an uncalled-for US$20, while visitors to Beng Melea have to shell out a reasonable US$5. The even more remote Koh Ker costs US$10.

Security

The Angkor Archaeological Park has been de-mined and robberies are virtually unheard of, making the area around the temples one of the safest places in Southeast Asia.

GETTING THERE AND AROUND

There are numerous ways to explore the temples of Angkor. The distance between the temples is too far to walk, not least because it's hot almost year-round, so it's best to have wheels of one sort or another.

For years, sitting on the back of a motorbike and having a local *motodup* take visitors around was the most common way to get around the Angkor Archaeological Park, and this is still possible. Daily rates are around US$8 and a tip is expected.

Tuk-tuks are becoming ever more popular, comfortably sit two (four people if necessary), and cost around US$15 a day. Note that for temples farther away from Siem Reap, such as Banteay Srei, higher rates apply. A taxi will set visitors back around US$30 per day; a mini-bus around US$50, more to the outlying temples. For more remote temples such as Preah Vihear, consider renting a Jeep or other four-wheel-drive, for around US$80. To reach Beng Melea and Koh Ker, from Siem Reap, a normal taxi is sufficient. Your hotel or guesthouse will be able to arrange all of these options.

An altogether different possibility is renting an electric bicycle, an option introduced in 2006. For US$4 a day, electric bikes can be rented on a small side road on the right-hand side of the road to Angkor, a few hundred meters before reaching the ticket booths. The bikes do a maximum of 30 kilometers with one charge; there are 14 charge points around the temples, so there's little danger of running out of juice. No doubt, these electric bikes leave the smallest carbon footprint—barring cycling, of course—but they take money out of the local economy. For every tourist who chooses to get around on an electric bike, a young *motodup* driver in Siem Reap loses a day's wages, some of the few tourist dollars that really trickle down to ordinary people, so crucial in one of Cambodia's poorest provinces.

VISITING THE TEMPLES

Most tourists follow the most logical routes, created by French archaeologists a hundred years ago: the **Petit Circuit,** the 17-kilometer short route, which leads past all the main temples. Alternatively, the **Grand Circuit,** the 26-kilometer long route, offers countryside vistas, but does not include some of the temple highlights, such as Ta Prohm. The temples of the Roluos Group are not part of either route and can be visited in a separate half-day excursion.

As one day is enough to time to complete the Petit Circuit, you might think that this is sufficient time to marvel at the temples. Indeed, it could be argued that visitors who spend just a single day amongst the ruins will have far less of an impact than three-day visitors. But perhaps too brief a glance at the Angkor temples, seen in passing as a series of monuments stuck in the dry soil of a poor country, does not do justice to Khmer culture and your own sense of discovery. To be sure, the majority of tourists who visit Angkor nowadays arrive as part of a package tour. They move about in air-conditioned buses, isolated from their environment, and when inside the temples, they are firmly tied to their guides and camcorders. In this sense, Angkor—like the pyramids of Giza,

CYCLE ANGKOR

Since many visitors have had motorcycle accidents on the roads around the temples, the local authorities have banned tourists from driving their own vehicles in Siem Reap. Bicycles are the exception to the rule.

The temple-park is ideal for cyclists, though on some of the roads between the main temples, tour-buses, taxis, and tuk-tuks cause traffic jams in the mornings and late afternoons. Generally, though, bicycles are the perfect alternative to motorized transportation, and are much more in tune with the magnificence of the temples and forest. All the roads between the temples are paved and there are no notable hills. While many of the roads lie in the shade of the forest, it does get infernally hot in the summertime, so make sure you drink plenty of water (available from stalls near every major temple) and use sunscreen. Also be sure you lock your bike anywhere you plan to leave it.

The ideal route is the 17-kilometer Petit Circuit, which starts at Angkor Wat, leads past Phnom Bakheng into Angkor Thom and past the Bayon, and leaves Angkor Thom towards Takeo and Ta Prohm before returning to Angkor Wat.

If you like the idea of a bike, but aren't too keen on cycling, the Angkor Archaeological Park might have just the thing for you – an electric bike. For US$4 a day, electric bikes can be rented a few hundred meters before reaching the ticket booths on the road to Angkor.

the Coliseum in Rome, and the Acropolis in Athens—has become part of the global archaeological tourist trench, traversed in the same manner by millions every year. Individual travelers can be more flexible and can take their time, giving the temples space to breathe and to fit into the country as a whole. Rather than tick off temple after temple, it might be worth lingering here and there. The atmosphere of each ruin changes significantly depending on the time of day, the light, and the numbers of visitors and local people present.

Exploring the temples with a guide can definitely enhance the experience and deepen your understanding of the magnificent civilization that once ruled over these buildings. The **Khmer Angkor Tour Guides Association (KATGA)** (tel. 063/964347, www.khmerangkortourguide.com) is the organization for official tour guides based in Siem Reap Angkor. The guides are trained by the Ministry of Tourism and the APSARA Authority. English- and French-speaking guides cost US$20–30 per day. Guides fluent in other languages, such as Spanish, German, or Japanese, are likely to cost more.

Your hotel or guesthouse will be able to arrange for an English-speaking guide for around US$30 a day. Note that tuk-tuk drivers and *motodups* are not allowed to guide tourists through the temples.

Numerous travel agents offer guided day tours for around US$60. This includes the US$20 entrance fee to the temples, as well as a guide, transport, and lunch. Sometimes a visit to the Angkor National Museum is also included. Three-day/two-night hotel and temple packages with pick-up from the airport, transport, accommodations, temple pass, and English-speaking guide cost around US$170–250, or more, depending on the cost of accommodations and the number of people in the group, and can also be booked through a local agent. If you book a tour as a group with a local travel agent, significant discounts are likely. Four-, five-, and six-day packages to the temples are also offered. Some tour operators make sure they benefit the local communities through their involvement with various aid projects.

Tour Operators

The following travel agents in Siem Reap offer standard tour packages for Angkor from one day to a week, as well as longer itineraries for locations further afield.

AboutAsia (tel. 092/121059, U.S. tel. 914/595-6949, www.asiatravel-cambodia.com)

runs tour packages around the temples and the country that involve the local community.

Angkor T.K. Travel & Tours (tel. 063/963320, www.angkortk.com) also runs tour packages around the temples as well as cycling tours.

The Villa Siem Reap (tel. 063/761036, www.thevillasiemreap.com) offers very competitive tours aimed at a young clientele; their popular five-night Siem Reap package for US$260 is a good value and good fun.

The World of Cambodia (tel. 063/963637, www.angkor-cambodia.org) has a wide selection of temple tours to suit all timetables and budgets, as well as hotel offers and tours further afield in Cambodia.

Souvenirs

In the unlikely event that you are offered anything that looks like antiques or genuine artifacts from the Angkor era, refuse to purchase these items; otherwise, you will become part of the international illegal trade of cultural artifacts. If you get caught at the airport with ancient carvings or even Buddha statues from the 19th century, you will certainly be arrested and charged.

Replicas of virtually every major structure or sculpture seen around the Angkor temples can be bought in Siem Reap and around some of the temples, made from virtually every material imaginable (including wood, bone, marble, and metal) and to suit all budgets. Groups of children sell drinks, wooden cowbells, T-shirts, and other small items in front of some of the ruins. They can be persistent, but bear in mind that the money they earn goes to the villages, rather than in the pockets of businessmen and the government. A number of musical instruments, including drums, and an ingenious mouth-harp made from bamboo and a fiddle, its sound body usually covered in snakeskin, are also offered in front of some of the temples.

APSARA, the nongovernmental organization in charge of the temples, has been making efforts to get rid of unregistered vendors and has even banned some older local monks from entering Angkor Wat, arguing that they might scare tourists.

◖ ANGKOR WAT

Angkor Wat, a Hindu temple or mausoleum, is the largest religious building in the world, and one of the most beautifully impressive structures built by humankind. It's up there with the pyramids and the Taj Mahal. Thousands labored for three decades to create this magnificent dream in stone. But this 12th-century temple is much more than its sublime architecture can convey: It is the heart and soul of Cambodia.

Most Cambodians have never had an opportunity to visit Angkor Wat, yet the temple represents the country's heritage and culture for every Khmer. Angkor Wat has been on every national flag in one shape or another since 1863. Since the mid-1990s, it has also become one of the world's best-known and most visited tourist sites. Angkor Wat means "royal monastery city," which is probably a variation on the Sanskrit word *nagara,* which means "capital." The word *wat* is Thai for "temple," and the term was probably added when the building became Buddhist.

I still vividly remember my first glimpse of the temple. I was riding a motorcycle along the wide tree-lined road from the ticket booths towards the temples, with a real air of excitement and anticipation. Monkeys swung from the trees and a couple of elephants stood in the shade, waiting for tourist passengers. Upon approaching the moat, I turned left, and followed the road that ran parallel to the dark green water towards the causeway. Suddenly, to my right and across the moat, I glimpsed, just for an instant, the massive central towers rising out of dense foliage. I remember it like a pleasant shock. A disbelief at form and dimension kicked in; the jungle ambience around me induced a real personal sense of discovery.

It's the sheer size, more than anything else, that throws the first-time visitor: The moat is 1.5 kilometers by 1.3 kilometers long and 200 meters wide, and it carries water to this day. Simply walking around the complex takes a couple of hours. The vastness of Angkor Wat makes it difficult to guess its exact shape, even as one stands on the causeway in front of the entry towers (take a few steps to your left, off the terrace that marks the start of the causeway, and you will be able to see all five towers). The causeway is 250 meters long and 12 meters wide. Without the benefit of elevation though, it's hard to fathom just how far—and in which directions—the building spreads out. The view from Phnom Bakheng gives visitors a pretty good idea as to its size. The rectangular shape of the temple spreads across 210 hectares.

Angkor Wat was built during and perhaps beyond the reign of Suryavarman II (1113–1150), and is thought to have served as a temple and a mausoleum. The latter is more likely, as Khmer temple gates usually face east. At Angkor, the main gate faces west.

Angkor Wat is a classic temple-mountain, a replica of the Hindu universe. The five towers represent the different peaks of Mount Meru, home to the Hindu pantheon, which sits in the center of the universe. The walls surrounding the sanctuary stand for the mountain ranges at the

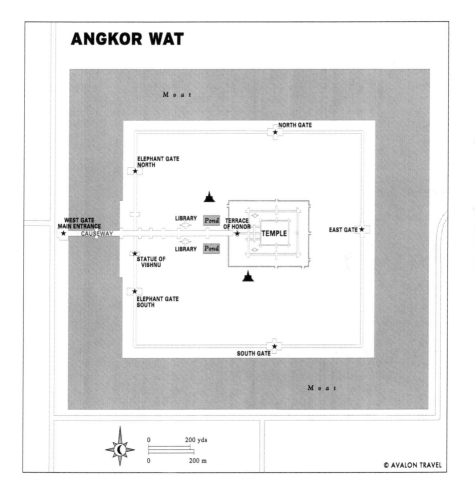

ANGKOR WAT

edge of the world. The moat symbolizes the cosmic ocean. Angor Wat was dedicated to Shiva, and many of the temple's proportions and architectural elements correspond to aspects of Hindu cosmology. Like many other classic-era Khmer temples, Angkor Wat was built from sandstone blocks and laterite.

After crossing the causeway, visitors reach the outer enclosure running along the western side of the compound in the shape of a gallery, pierced by five entrances. Three towers, partially collapsed, sit on top of the enclosure. Underneath the central tower, a *gopura* (entrance hall) serves as an antechamber to the inner courtyard of the enclosure. Immediately to the right, inside the enclosure, rests a large statue of the Buddha, usually with a couple of old ladies in attendance lighting incense. As you step through the *gopura,* Angkor Wat rises straight ahead, at the end of another raised promenade, 350 meters long and 9 meters wide, that leads across open ground past two small libraries and a couple of lotus ponds. The magnitude of the building really becomes obvious as you approach

the sanctuary along this promenade. The pond on the right usually contains more water than the one on the left and is a great place to get atmospheric shots of Angkor in the late afternoon. Locals offer tourists the chance to sit on a horse and have their picture taken. Surprisingly, they get quite a few customers.

Angkor Wat is built on three levels, each one smaller and higher than the last, culminating in the 65-meter-high central tower.

The First Level

The **Terrace of Honor** connects the promenade to the first level, which is framed by galleries on all sides facing outwards. The galleries contain incredible bas-reliefs that cover almost all of the inner wall space. Ignoring those for the moment, and approaching from the promenade and walking straight on towards the central tower, visitors pass by two inner galleries, both in the shape of a cross.

To the left, the **Hall of Echoes** has great acoustics, if you manage to get a moment alone inside. To the right, the **Gallery of a**

apsara dancers carved on the wall of the outer enclosure around Angkor Wat

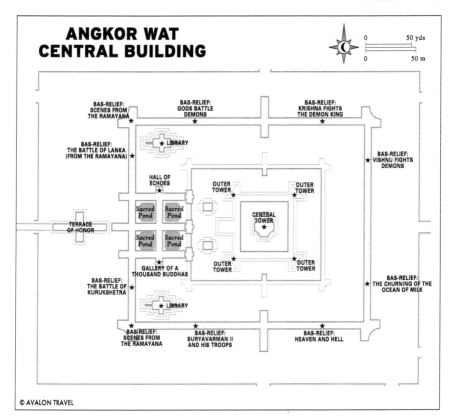

ANGKOR WAT CENTRAL BUILDING

0 — 50 yds
0 — 50 m

BAS-RELIEF: SCENES FROM THE RAMAYANA

BAS-RELIEF: GODS BATTLE DEMONS

BAS-RELIEF: KRISHNA FIGHTS THE DEMON KING

BAS-RELIEF: THE BATTLE OF LANKA (FROM THE RAMAYANA)

LIBRARY

BAS-RELIEF: VISHNU FIGHTS DEMONS

HALL OF ECHOES

OUTER TOWER

OUTER TOWER

TERRACE OF HONOR

Sacred Pond *Sacred Pond*

CENTRAL TOWER

Sacred Pond *Sacred Pond*

GALLERY OF A THOUSAND BUDDHAS

OUTER TOWER

OUTER TOWER

BAS-RELIEF: THE BATTLE OF KURUKSHETRA

LIBRARY

BAS-RELIEF: THE CHURNING OF THE OCEAN OF MILK

BAS-RELIEF: SCENES FROM THE RAMAYANA

BAS-RELIEF: SURYAVARMAN II AND HIS TROOPS

BAS-RELIEF: HEAVEN AND HELL

Thousand Buddhas did once contain many Buddha statues from the 14th century, a time when the Khmer Empire had permanently converted to Buddhism.

Beyond these two galleries, four courtyards with basins for ritual bathing feature windows with stone balusters made to look as if they'd been carved from wood, as well as a frieze of *apsaras*. The pillars around the pools feature Khmer and Sanskrit inscriptions.

THE BAS-RELIEFS

One of the highlights of visiting Angkor Wat, if not Cambodia, are the bas-reliefs that spread all around the galleries. Two meters high, this narrative in stone covers 1,200 square meters with kings and battles, gods and demons,

heaven and hell, and the greatest stories from Hindu mythology.

Like a graphic novel for giants, drawn with incredible grace, an amazing eye for detail and atmosphere, the bas-reliefs are like a window into another world. The pillars that support the gallery roofs at regular intervals throw shadow patterns across the images that only enhance their energy. The bas-reliefs of Angkor Wat are truly a repository of sublime art, a testament to human creativity. Some of the bas-reliefs look like they have been polished. This could be due to them having been painted or because many people ran their hands over them.

Moving counter-clockwise from the Terrace of Honor:

The Battle of Kurukshetra: The southern

part of the western gallery depicts the battle of Kurukshetra, part of the *Mahabharata,* a Hindu epic, in which the clans of Kaurava and Pandava annihilate each other. The two armies march towards one another from opposite ends of the relief and clash in its center amongst elephants and chariots ridden by officers. Arrows fly in all directions and troops are engaged in bloody, close-quarters combat.

Scenes from the *Ramayana* (southwest): The pavilion on the southwestern corner contains a bas-relief depicting scenes from the *Ramayana,* another famous Hindu epic (the Khmer version is the *Reamker*), including Krishna lifting Mount Govardhana in order to defeat Indra. Some of the reliefs in this pavilion were damaged by leaks.

Suryavarman II and His Troops: The western part of the southern gallery features a historical scene, with Suryavarman II, the Khmer king who built Angkor Wat, sitting under royal parasols, inspecting his army and getting ready for battle.

Heaven and Hell: The eastern part of the southern gallery is nothing short of brutal. Yama, the god of hell, judges divides mankind into those who move upwards to heaven or downwards, through a trap door, into hell, where they are tortured, maimed, and killed over and over. The scenes of men with whips pushing endless chains of the condemned ahead of them seem like macabre visions of Cambodia's more recent past.

The Churning of the Ocean of Milk: On the southern side of the eastern gallery, the greatest of all the reliefs depicts one of the most important Hindu myths: the churning of the ocean of milk. Ninety-two *asuras* (demons) on the left and eighty-eight *devas* (gods) on the right grab the serpent Vasuki at opposite ends and pull back and forth for a thousand years, as they try to produce *amrita,* the nectar of immortality. The serpent coils around Mount Meru, which serves as the implement to churn the ocean. Gods and demons stretch across the entire panel. Above them, *apsaras* dance in the heavens. A four-armed Vishnu dances in the center of the panel. A demon king holds the

detail of the Suryavarman II and His Troops bas-relief on the western side of Angkor Wat's southern gallery

head of the serpent while the god of monkeys, Hanuman, holds its tail high over the *devas'* heads. Below the temple mount and the dancing Vishnu, Kurma, a reincarnation of Vishnu in the shape of a tortoise, provides a solid base in the churning ocean for Mount Meru to rest on. Mythical sea creatures swim around the bottom of the panel.

Vishnu Fights Demons: The northern part of the eastern gallery depicts Vishnu doing battle with innumerable demons. This relief is most likely of a later date, probably produced in the 16th century, somewhat less sublime than the main panels in this gallery, but still captivating.

Krishna Fights the Demon King: The eastern part of the northern gallery shows Krishna riding a *garuda.* Bana, the demon king, arrives from the opposite side. Krishna is stopped short by a burning city, Bana's home, but finally overcomes the demon with the help of the *garuda,* who manages to extinguish the flame.

Gods Battle Demons: On the western side of the northern gallery, a battle between gods and demons rages. The 21 Brahman gods all ride their traditional mounts—such as Brahma riding a goose and Vishnu mounted on a *garuda*.

Scenes from the *Ramayana* (northwest): In the northwestern pavilion, as in the southwestern pavilion, scenes from the *Ramayana* are played out, including a depiction of Vishnu with his wife Lakshmi by his feet, and numerous *apsaras* floating above his head.

The Battle of Lanka: The northern part of the western gallery displays a key scene from the *Ramayana,* the battle of Lanka, in which Rama fights with the demon king Ravana in order to claim his wife, who has been abducted to Lanka. In order to win the fierce battle, Rama calls upon the services of Hanuman, god of the monkeys, who attacks Ravana as the demon god rides a huge chariot and commands an army of brutal warriors. Once past this amazing tableau, the Terrace of Honor is just ahead.

The Second Level

Moving east from the galleries on the first level, steps lead to the second level. Its outside wall is undecorated, but on the inside, more than 1,500 *apsaras* vie for the attention of everyone passing. Alone or in small groups, each of the celestial dancers is slightly different from the next and it is hard to imagine a space more intent on celebrating the sensuousness of female beauty.

The Third Level

The third level was off-limits to all but the king and his high priest. It forms the base that the five towers, which represent the peaks of Mount Meru, stand on (with four of the towers on the corners and the fifth right in the center).

The views from the very top reveal the symmetrical nature of the temple complex and drive home what a wonder this building is. The third level is framed by an open gallery, which affords great views across the surrounding forest. Libraries, courtyards, and stairways surround the central tower, which rises 42 meters above the third level and 65 meters above the

ground. Originally, the small sanctuary underneath the tower housed a statue of Vishnu. Today, locals light incense in front of a contemporary Buddha statue here.

The stairs up the central tower, which ascend at an awe-inspiring 40 percent angle, can no longer be climbed, for fear of accidents. Plans to build a wooden stairway have yet to materialize.

◖ ANGKOR THOM

The crowning achievement of Jayavarman VII, the greatest of all the Khmer kings, was the construction of Angkor Thom, his "Great City," in the late 12th and early 13th centuries. Spread over an area of 10 square kilometers, this massive settlement is likely to have once supported a population of some one million people. It is surrounded by an eight-meter-high laterite wall, three kilometers long on each side, as well as 100-meter-wide moat.

Visitors enter via wide causeways that lead through five giant gates, crowned by *gopuras,* facing the cardinal directions (the eastern wall has two gates, the East Gate and the Gate of Victory, which connects the temple of Ta Prohm to the Terraces of the Leper King and Elephants), with four impassive faces of the *bodhisattva,* the enlightened one, staring at everyone arriving and departing.

The causeways are lined by two balustrades formed by 54 gods on the left and 54 demons to the right, with each group holding a *naga* snake, a reference to the Churning of the Ocean of Milk, the Hindu myth at the heart of Khmer culture. The roads running through the main gates all lead towards the Bayon, at the very center of Angkor Thom. The entire city is a representation of the Hindu universe, with the walls and moat symbolizing the mountain ranges and cosmic ocean surrounding Mount Meru.

The royal entourage, from the king down to the priests and generals, lived within the city walls, while the commoners lived in wooden houses, probably much like traditional Khmer houses today, beyond the outer enclosure.

In the heart of Angkor Thom, the Terrace of the Elephants and the Terrace of the Leper

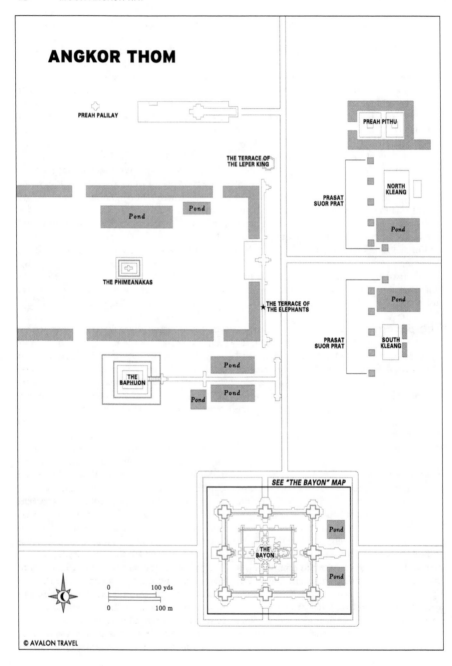

ANGKOR THOM

PREAH PALILAY

PREAH PITHU

THE TERRACE OF
THE LEPER KING

NORTH
KLEANG

PRASAT
SUOR PRAT

Pond

Pond

Pond

THE PHIMEANAKAS

★ THE TERRACE OF
THE ELEPHANTS

Pond

PRASAT
SUOR PRAT

SOUTH
KLEANG

Pond

THE
BAPHUON

Pond

Pond

Pond

SEE "THE BAYON" MAP

Pond

THE
BAYON

Pond

0   100 yds

0   100 m

© AVALON TRAVEL

© AROON THAEWCHATTURAT

The causeway to the south gate of Angkor Thom is lined with 54 heads of gods and demons.

King are most likely the foundations of a palace complex. The royal buildings were built from wood and no one is sure what they looked like. Nevertheless, the structures that are left give an impression as to the grandeur of Angkor Thom, the last great capital of the Khmer Empire.

The Bayon

More than 200 faces on 54 towers stare down at the world with what the French termed the *sourir Khmer* (the smile of the Khmer). Ambivalent, compassionate, and cruel at the same time, enigmatic for its mystery, the smile follows every visitor around the temple building, which is second in popularity only to Angkor Wat.

Some researchers believe the faces belong to the *bodhisattva* Avalokitshvara. Others think they represent the king himself: powerful, terrible, and compassionate, his eyes set on even the most remote parts of a vast kingdom at any given time. Perhaps both interpretations are true. What's sure is that visitors can feel the stares of the impassive faces wherever they are

inside the Bayon. Jayavarman VII was truly a Big Brother of antiquity.

The history of the Bayon is shrouded in as much mystery as the famous smiles on its towers. The temple was built on top of an older structure and was initially dated to the 9th century. It was discovered to be a Buddhist structure only in 1925, and the fact that the Bayon is at the exact center of the great city also eluded visitors for a long time. After the death of Jayavarman VII, who followed Mahayana Buddhism, the temple served as a Hindu and later Theravada Buddhist institution.

The Bayon is built on three levels. Incredible bas-reliefs cover some of the walls of the first and second levels, while the third level is dominated by the 54 towers and the central sanctuary. On the first level, an outer gallery is marked by eight *gopuras,* four of them at each corner and another four constructed at the middle point of each gallery. Inside the gallery of the first level, a couple of libraries can be found in the eastern courtyards.

The second level is bordered by another gallery, marked by four towers on the corners

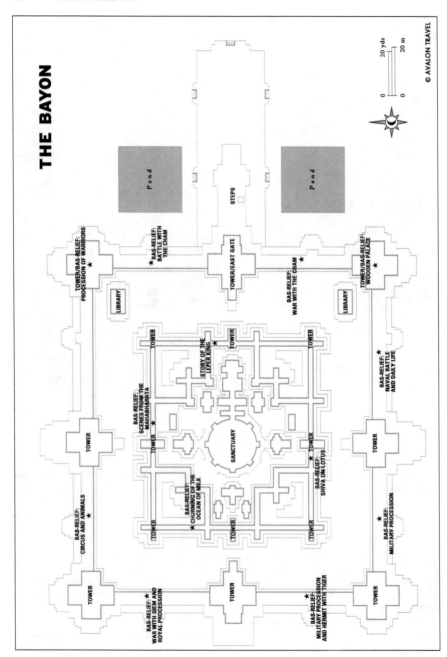

THE BAYON

20 yds

20 m

© AVALON TRAVEL

Pond

Pond

STEPS

TOWER/BAS-RELIEF:
PROCESSION OF WARRIORS

BAS-RELIEF:
BATTLE WITH
THE CHAM

TOWER/EAST GATE

BAS-RELIEF:
WAR WITH THE CHAM

TOWER/BAS-RELIEF:
WOODEN PALACE

LIBRARY

LIBRARY

TOWER

TOWER

STORY OF THE
LEPER KING

TOWER

BAS-RELIEF:
SCENES FROM THE
MAHABHARATA

TOWER

SANCTUARY

TOWER

BAS-RELIEF:
NAVAL BATTLE
AND DAILY LIFE

TOWER

BAS-RELIEF:
CHURNING OF THE
OCEAN OF MILK

TOWER

BAS-RELIEF:
SHIVA ON LOTUS

TOWER

TOWER

BAS-RELIEF:
CIRCUS AND ANIMALS

BAS-RELIEF:
MILITARY PROCESSION

TOWER

TOWER

TOWER

BAS-RELIEF:
WAR WITH SIEM AND
ROYAL PROCESSION

BAS-RELIEF:
MILITARY PROCESSION
AND HERMIT WITH TIGER

© AROON THAEWCHATTURAT

one of the more than 200 carved faces that dominate the Bayon, the state temple in the center of Angkor Thom

and four *gopuras,* again at the middle point of each gallery. Quite a bit of the second level has collapsed and as you scramble across boulders and take small detours, it's easy to lose your orientation. Restoration work may also make access to some areas of the second level a little difficult.

The third level is circular in shape, unusual in Khmer temple architecture, and contains the faces of the *bodhisattva* Avalokitshvara arranged around the temple's central sanctuary.

THE BAS-RELIEFS

The incredible bas-reliefs of the Bayon cover an area of some 1.2 kilometers. The Bayon's main entrance faces east and the main bas-reliefs are briefly described starting from here, moving clockwise, with the reliefs on the right.

First Level

The reliefs on the first level were accessible to ordinary people and offer visitors a rare glimpse of what daily life for Cambodians must have

been like during the Angkor era. Perhaps they served educational purposes: to inform the people of the merits of Buddhism. Some reliefs were never finished.

War with the Cham: The southern part of the eastern gallery is divided into three tiers and shows the Cambodian army on its way home, victorious after fighting the Cham. On the lowest tier, the army, moving on elephants and ox-carts, and accompanied by musicians, returns to Angkor. On the far right, Chinese traders can be seen. In the middle tier, fallen soldiers are returned home, and on the top tier, Jayavarman VII, protected by a parasol, heads a procession along with his commanders, on the back of an elephant.

Wooden Palace: The southeast corner pavilion contains unfinished reliefs of a wooden palace and a boat.

Naval Battle and Daily Life: The eastern part of the southern gallery is dedicated to the naval battle between the Khmer and the Cham that took place on the Tonlé Sap Lake in 1177. On the right, most easterly panel, hunters, men playing chess, women searching for head lice, and musicians are depicted on a lower tier. On the left panel, the battle is fierce and some soldiers are eaten by crocodiles after they have fallen into the water. On a lower tier, a woman gives birth, food is prepared, and another game of chess is in progress.

Military Procession: The western part of the southern gallery was never completed, though it does show a military procession, complete with crossbow-wielding soldiers mounted on elephants, as well as a sophisticated catapult on wheels.

Military Procession and Hermit with Tiger: The southern part of the western gallery is unfinished and shows a military procession passing through mountainous countryside, as well as a hermit climbing a tree to escape an attacking tiger. Farther on, a stand-off between two crowds is about to spill over into violence.

War with Siem and Royal Procession: The northern part of the western gallery contains scenes of close-up fighting between the Khmer

© AROON THAEWCHATTURAT

detail of the Naval Battle and Daily Life bas-relief on the Bayon's first level

and the Siamese, as well as a procession of the king on his way to meditate in the forest.

Circus and Animals: The northern gallery features a circus in its far-right corner, including jugglers and acrobats, while the royal court looks on. A procession of animals includes the now-extinct rhinoceros, as well as a pig, rabbit, deer, fish, and lobster. There's also a scene of meditating holy men in the forest and a group of women by a river receiving gifts.

Procession of Warriors: The northeast corner pavilion features yet another processions of warriors and their pachyderm rides.

Khmer Battle with the Cham: In the northern section of the eastern gallery, the Khmer appear to be gaining on the Cham in battle and even the elephants rip into each other.

Second Level

The bas-reliefs on the second inner level were accessible only to the king and his priests and feature scenes from Hindu mythology, as well as a few depictions of battle and everyday scenes. Given that Jayavarman VII introduced Mahayan Buddhism to the Khmer Empire,

this seems somewhat incongruous. But many things about the Bayon are not fully understood yet. The reliefs on the second level appear to either pre-date the rest of the temple by several hundred years—and were from the time of Yasovarman I, a Hindu king who ruled at the end of the 9th century—or they post-date Jayavarman VII's reign and were placed in the Bayon by Jayavarman VIII, a Hindu king, during the late 13th century. The panels of the inner galleries, separated by doors and towers, are smaller, not in as good condition, and are more fragmented than those on the outside.

Starting from the eastern entrance again, some of the highlights include several depictions of **Shiva** in the southern gallery; the **Churning of the Ocean of Milk** in the northern part of the western gallery; Shiva in several **scenes from the *Mahabharata*** on the eastern side of the north gallery; and the **story of the leper king,** which depicts a king being bitten while fighting a snake, then being observed and treated by a holy man and surrounded by women who examine his hands—just to the right of the main entrance in the eastern gallery.

The Baphuon

The Baphuon, a classic temple-mountain representing Mount Meru, was built in the 11th century, and therefore precedes Angkor Thom. Originally a Hindu temple, dedicated to Shiva, the Baphuon adjoins the royal palace enclosure. Its base measures 120 meters by 100 meters, and it's about 35 meters tall, minus its tower, which has collapsed. On its western side's second level, a reclining Buddha, nine meters tall and 70 meters long, was constructed in the 15th century.

In the 1960s, the EFEO began the huge reconstruction process, using the method of anastylosis, a technique that calls for the total dismantling and subsequent rebuilding of a structure. Unfortunately, by the time the Khmer Rouge made work on the temple impossible in 1972, this immense undertaking was unfinished and the plans were lost in the chaos that ensued. What was left was a sea of stones lying around in a loosely organized fashion.

The challenge of rebuilding the temple was taken up in 1995 and was still ongoing in 2009, though some parts of the temple, which contain interesting bas-reliefs, have become accessible once more.

The Phimeanakas

The Phimeanakas is a 10th-century temple-mountain close to the royal palace area of Angkor Thom. The central tower has collapsed and the three original levels have long been looted of its architectural subtleties. The royal enclosure too is largely in ruins. The royal palace would have been built from wood and there's no consensus on what it might have looked like.

The Terrace of the Elephants

This 350-meter-long terrace was once covered in wooden pavilions. From here, Jayavarman VII could inspect his troops as they marched into Angkor Thom from the Victory Gate. The terrace takes its name from the carved elephants on its eastern side and faces a central square where the troops would have marched in procession.

Carvings of lions and *garudas* can be found on the middle section of the terrace's retaining wall.

The Terrace of the Leper King

The jury is still out as to whether the 15th-century statue found on top of this platform to the north of the Terrace of the Elephants is a Khmer king with leprosy, or Yama, the Hindu god of death. The outer walls of the terrace are covered in reliefs of mythical beings and *apsaras*. The structure might have served as the royal crematorium. Most interestingly, there is a hidden inner wall on the terrace's south side. Visitors can walk along a narrow corridor crammed with several tiers of carved scenes in pristine condition, including *apsaras, nagas,* elephants, and a river with fish.

Other Structures

Many other ruins are dotted around the enormous enclosure of Angkor Thom. **Preah Palilay** is a small atmospheric Buddhist temple located to the north of the royal enclosure, erected during the reign of Jayavarman VII, with a chimney-like tower. Facing the Terrace of the Elephants across the central square, two so-called *kleangs* (the somewhat misleading Khmer word for storeroom) may have once served as royal guesthouses. The *kleangs* are older than Angkor Thom and were probably built in the 10th century. They are fronted by **Prasat Suor Prat,** a series of 12 laterite towers. Also built by Jayavarman VII, the towers once housed sacred statues or linga.

To the north of the *kleangs,* **Preah Pithu** is a group of five small temples, most of them Buddhist. Not too many visitors bother to come here and the atmosphere is very peaceful and relaxed.

THE TEMPLES OF ANGKOR
Phnom Wat Bakheng

Wat Bakheng was the very first temple-mountain constructed in the Angkor area. Dating back to the late 9th century, this Hindu temple marked the move from the smaller capitals around Roluos and sat at the

ANGKOR FROM THE AIR

Fancy a totally different view of the temples? Try Angkor from above. In all, there are three different possibilities to see Angkor from the air, each with their own merits.

The most straightforward way is to search for the **yellow balloon** (tel. 012/520810) that is tethered near Angkor Wat, on the road to the airport, and jump on board. The balloon (US$11 per person) rises to a height of 200 meters and the views of Angkor Wat, Phnom Bakheng, and the surrounding countryside are impressive.

Far more exclusive and expensive, but even more breathtaking, is a ride in a helicopter. Two outfits currently offer scenic flights starting at US$50 a head. **Sokha Helicopters** (tel. 016/731468, www. sokhahelicopters.com) is stationed right next to the big yellow balloon, while **Helicopters Cambodia** (tel. 012/814500, www. helicoterscambodia.com), a New Zealand outfit with an excellent safety track record, is based at the airport.

Finally, for those with high-altitude vertigo, a ride on an **elephant** may suffice. You still get better views than on foot, but there's no need to rise to extreme heights. During the day, elephants can be hired around the Bayon. In the afternoon, they tend to move to Phnom Bakheng in order to take visitors to this hilltop temple for the sunset. A 30-minute ride costs US$10-15.

heart of the royal capital of Yasodharapura. The temple's base is carved from the mountain itself and the climb up the front stairway is steep. Nevertheless, Wat Bakheng is the most popular sunset spot in the Angkor Archaeological Park and attracts thousands of visitors every night because it has fine views of Tonlé Sap Lake and Angkor Wat peeking out of the surrounding forest.

Elephant rides to the top are available (US$15). Rumors of an escalator to be constructed have persisted for years. Let's hope it will never happen.

Baksei Chamkrong

Located north of Phnom Bakheng, Baksei Chamkrong is a small but attractive pyramid-shaped temple built in the mid-10th century, just after the Khmer capital returned from Koh Ker to the Angkor area. The structure was originally dedicated to Shiva. Built from bricks and laterite, it has some sandstone decorations and is 12 meters tall.

Baksei Chamkrong means "the bird that shelters under its wings," a reference to a story about a Khmer king trying to flee Angkor as his city was besieged by a foreign army. A giant bird suddenly swooped from the sky and took the king under its wings, protecting him from the onslaught.

Thomanon

A contemporary of Angkor Wat, the small but graciously designed Thomanon was built in the early 12th century under the reign of Suryavarman II, and similarities are especially apparent in the design of the towers. Extensive restoration work in the 1960s did wonders for this Hindu temple, located on the left side of the road, just outside the Victory Gate on the way to Ta Keo.

Chaosay Tevoda

Just across the road from the Thomanon, this small temple has a similar floor plan and looks like it was built in conjunction. In fact, Chaosay Tevoda was built some years later. It features additional *gopuras* and a library, and is slowly being restored.

Ta Keo

A few hundred meters east of the Victory Gate, Ta Keo is a towering, unadorned temple pyramid that rises above the canopy of the surrounding forest. Built in the early 11th century during the reign of Jayavarman V from massive sandstone blocks, Ta Keo, facing east and dedicated to Shiva, was never completed, for reasons unknown. The total lack of decorations,

Ta Keo, an unadorned temple pyramid that was never completed

reliefs or otherwise, gives this temple a unique singularly powerful appearance—it seems built like a fortress. Nevertheless, the steep climb to the top, via any of the four stairways at the cardinal points, is worth the effort. The views across the trees are great and the ambience between the five towers up top is somehow quietly dignified, perhaps because not very many people come up here.

◖ Ta Prohm

More than any other major monument in the Angkor Archaeological Park, Ta Prohm is a trip back in time. When the French began to push the jungle back from the ruins at the beginning of the 20th century, the EFEO decided, for aesthetic reasons, that one temple should be left in its forest context, just the way French explorers had stumbled upon the ruins some 50 years prior to that. And that's the reason why some scenes of the movie *Tomb Raider* were shot inside the temple.

Of course, much work has been done on this huge sprawling temple complex and the jungle around the site has long been well managed—though several large silk cottonwood and strangler fig trees have enormous roots sprouting across boulders and galleries, giving the site its unique Lost World feel.

Ta Prohm is a very handsome temple, built in the late 12th and early 13th centuries by the greatest of the Khmer kings, Jayavarman VII, to serve as a Mahayana Buddhism monastery and university. The rectangular temple complex is not a temple-mountain like Angkor Wat and is therefore not built in ascending levels. The temple sanctuary is surrounded by five walls and a series of long and low buildings. The outermost laterite wall is 1,000 by 700 meters long and the entire complex is 650,000 square meters in size.

In the 13th century, it was home to more than 12,000 people, including 18 high priests, 2,700 officials, and more than 600 dancers—with another 80,000 people living in 3,000 villages outside its walls to provide services. But the temple's possessions extended well beyond serfdom: Ta Prohm's vaults were said to hold more than 500 kilograms of golden dishes, 35 diamonds, 40,000 pearls, and 500 silk beds.

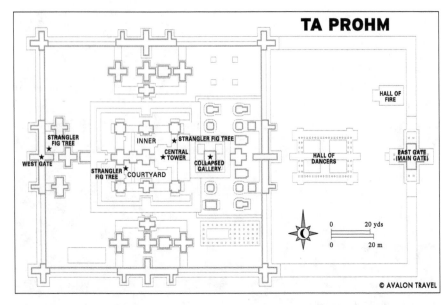

The monastic study center was a powerful concern indeed. Four *gopuras,* with heads similar to those on top the towers at the Bayon, provided access through the outermost wall into the complex, though today only the east and west entrance are open. Access is generally from the west, so most visitors get in via the back door. Have your driver drop you off at the eastern *gopura* and enter the temple the way it was designed to be entered.

Much of the ground between the fifth and fourth wall is overgrown by brush and large trees, but in its time, it must have been a small city, with wooden homes for the many staff. Two moats, on both sides of the fourth wall, have long dried up.

There are few bas-reliefs on the walls of Ta Prohm. Scholars speculate that these might have been destroyed, following Jayavarman VII's death and Angkor's reconversion to Hinduism, though there are some carvings of Buddhist iconography. Some of the *apsaras* had their heads cut off by looters many years ago. Several independent buildings stand freely within the complex. In the outermost enclosure, a **Hall of Fire,** a rest house or the home of a sacred flame,

stands alone to the east of the sanctuary. In the eastern part of the fourth enclosure, a **Hall of Dancers,** a structure Jayavarman VII had built in several of his temple complexes, features carvings of dancing *apsaras.* The central sanctuary is entirely unadorned. Its walls may have once been covered in silver.

But it's not so much the temple itself, though vast and gracious, as the interplay between stone and forest, that impresses visitors so much. And as many walls, corridors, and galleries have collapsed because of the jungle's intrusion, the temple's layout does not become apparent, because of the circuitous route visitors take. Several stretches of ground within the three central enclosures are so strewn with boulders that wooden walkways have been erected to make progress easier, and visitors are strongly discouraged to climb across collapsed walls. As Ta Prohm is afforded more shade by the forest than the other major monuments, the temple is not a bad place to visit when the sun is high up.

The scholar Claude Jacques remarked that Ta Prohm, more than any other Khmer temple, tempted writers into descriptive excess. Enough said.

the partially overgrown temple of Ta Prohm

Banteay Kdei

Just to the southeast of Ta Prohm, Banteay Kdei, built during the reign of Jayavarman VII, is yet another temple complex that served as a monastery. Due to inferior building materials, large parts of this temple have collapsed and much of the Buddhist imagery was vandalized in the 13th century, following the death of Jayavarman VII and the brief return of Angkor to Hinduism.

Banteay Kdei lies opposite Sra Srang, a reservoir that holds water year-round. In the dry season, a small island temple can be seen poking through the water's surface.

Prasat Kravan

This 10th-century Hindu temple was reconstructed by the French in the 19th century and sports its five original towers. Located to the south of Ta Prohm on the road back to Angkor Wat, Prasat Kravan was built from brick. Its interiors feature the only brick bas-reliefs in the Angkor area—notably depictions of Vishnu riding a *garuda* in the central tower, and Lakshmi holding the trident of Shiva and the discus of Vishnu in the northernmost tower. Few visitors stop here and while it's not the most atmospheric location, the reliefs are worth checking out.

Pre Rup

Situated to the south of the Eastern Baray, Pre Rup, along with the Eastern Mebon, was one of the first temples built by King Rajendravarman II, after the capital moved back to Angkor from Koh Ker in the late 10th century. Pre Rup, Rajendravarman II's state temple, is a classic temple-mountain with five towers on a raised platform, dedicated to Shiva.

Built from red brick, laterite, and sandstone, the temple sits amidst two enclosure walls. Within the walls, the temple rests on a main platform built on three levels. Right in front of the temple within the outer wall and facing east, six towers flank the entrance. One tower, on the immediate right as you enter the complex, might never have been built or has been demolished. The second enclosure is entered

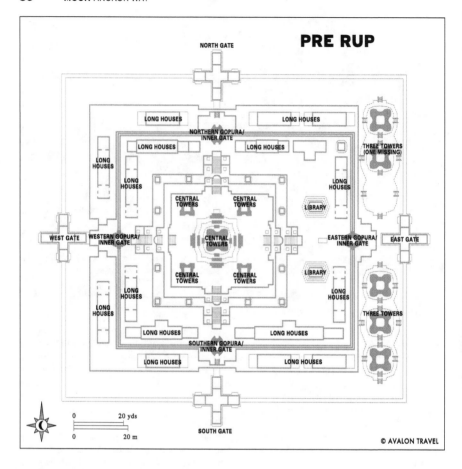

via four small *gopuras* at the cardinal points and contains several long houses, perhaps resting places for pilgrims. Two libraries with large towers are located just inside the courtyard entered through the eastern *gopura*.

The central platform of Pre Rup, split into three levels, is accessed via four stairways leading up from the *gopuras*. Next to the stairways, stone lions stand guard. The first two levels are built from laterite, while the third, top-most level is constructed from sandstone. On the first level, numerous small shrines containing linga, stand facing east. The five central towers on the third level, one in each corner and one in the center of the top platform, contain some interesting bas-reliefs, notably Vishnu and his avatar, as well as flying *apsaras*.

Eastern Mebon

The construction of the Eastern Mebon precedes that of Pre Rup by a decade and the similarity in building style is obvious. The Eastern Mebon was the very first temple constructed by Rajendravarman II after the Khmer capital moved back from Koh Ker to Angkor, and was dedicated to his parents. It follows the same design as Pre Rup: It's a temple-mountain dedicated to Shiva, surrounded

PRESERVATION, BUSINESS, AND THE THEFT
OF ANCIENT ARTIFACTS AT ANGKOR

When the Siamese sacked Angkor in 1431, they took whatever they could chisel off the walls with them. Ever since, the temples of the Angkor Empire have been looted – and Cambodia's cultural heritage continues to be plundered to this day.

After the Siamese, the Burmese looted Angkor in the 16th century and took more statues with them. In the 1870s, some years after Cambodia had become a French protectorate and Henri Mouhot had rediscovered the ruins, another Frenchman, Louis Delaporte, on an exploratory mission to the temples, took a wealth of statues and lintels back to France, where they can be seen at the Musée Guimet in Paris to this day. While this was sanctioned by the French government, the plan by the French writer André Malraux, who later became Minister of Culture in France, to steal several important pieces from Banteay Srei backfired when he was arrested for the trafficking of antiquities and thrown in jail. Malraux's connections soon got him out of this predicament though. In 1925, the area around the temples was declared a national park and looting subsided for a few years – until the chaos of World War II brought new opportunities for thieves; priceless objects disappeared in large numbers until Cambodia's independence in 1953. As the country slid into the Vietnam conflict in the late 1960s, a trickle of artifacts continued to move across its borders; following the Vietnamese liberation in 1979, the Khmer Rouge, who had retreated to the Cambodian Thai border, not far from the temples, engaged in the smuggling of statues.

But the worst was yet to come. As UNTAC moved into Cambodia in the early 1990s and the country's borders opened once more, the temples became accessible to an unprecedented wave of professional looters, some of them Cambodian police or military, who stole specific items for wealthy overseas collectors, destroying many significant structures that had weathered 800 years since being abandoned. The audacious removal of an entire temple wall from Banteay Chhmar near Sisophon in 1998 is one of the best-known examples of these widespread activities. Cambodian military spent four weeks carving the desired stones out of the temple with circular saws – luckily, in this case, the priceless carvings were intercepted at the Thai border and returned to Cambodia. Several American and European museums have also returned statues, and the United States and other countries have banned the import of Cambodian antiquities.

Looting also takes place on a smaller, less professional scale. Villagers or road builders sometimes come across temple structures and burial sites. In 2001, I passed through the village of Phum Snay, near Poipet. Within days of the discovery of a number pre-Angkorian graves, the local people had dug up their entire village, under the guidance of a foreigner who photographed and bagged each item found. The smuggler disappeared with the best pieces, and for weeks afterwards, locals stood by the roadside selling beads, precious stones, and pottery, until the site was entirely depleted.

As long as poverty is widespread in Cambodia, no amount of public campaigning or education will stop people from digging up and selling their national heritage for a few dollars.

by two walls, constructed on three levels, and crowned by five towers. The temple is built from a combination of brick, laterite, and sandstone, much like other early Angkorian structures. Impressive two-meter-high stone elephants guard the corners of the first and second levels. The towers were once covered in stucco. Today it's the red brick originally underneath, best photographed in the late afternoon, that's visible. Several lintels are covered in impressive carvings with themes from the Hindu pantheon.

It was built on an artificial island in the middle of the Eastern Baray, which is now dry. The Eastern Mebon stands just 1,200 meters to the north of Pre Rup on a direct north–south axis, and 6,800 meters to the east of the royal temple-mountain of Phimeanakas, on a direct east–west axis.

Neak Pean

Part of the Grand Circuit, Neak Pean is small, a bit out of the way, and otherworldly beautiful. Located to the east of Preah Khan on a direct east–west axis, this modest island temple was designed as an oasis of peace and reflection—part of a hospital constructed during the reign of Jayavarman VII, and hence dedicated to Buddha.

Neak Pean stands in the center of the Jayatataka Baray, which measured 3.5 kilometers by 900 meters and could only be reached by boat in its day. Today the reservoir is dry. In fact, Neak Pean stands on an island within a pond. The pond is surrounded by four more, smaller ponds. Four pavilions stand between the central pond and these smaller ponds, once used by pilgrims to absolve themselves of their sins. In each pavilion, a waterspout in the shape of a head conveyed water from the main pool into the smaller pools. There's an elephant head in the northern pavilion, a human head in the eastern one, a lion's head in the southern one, and a horse's head in the western one. These smaller ponds represent the elements of water, earth, wind, and fire, and it is thought that people with illnesses came to bathe here to reattain their natural balance with nature. Neak Pean was a Khmer spa. The entire complex sits in a walled enclosure, which in turn is located on an island in the *baray*. Access is from the north via a pier the French built.

Neak Pean, which means "entwined serpents," got its name from the two *naga* snakes that coil around the central island, which is round. The heads of the two snakes are separated, facing each other, and form an entrance to the sanctuary. The sculpture of a horse appears to be swimming away from the temple on its eastern side. The horse is a manifestation of the *bodhisattva* Avalokitshvara and was rebuilt from fragments by the EFEO during the temple's restoration in the 1920s.

Sometimes a group of blind musicians sits under the bushes by the side of the pond and plays, lending this little location even more atmosphere. Neak Pean is best visited just after the rainy season in October or November, when some of the ponds may contain some water.

Ta Som

Also worth a visit is the northeastern-most temple on the Grand Circuit, the small and peaceful Ta Som. Built like a miniature version of Ta Prohm, and dedicated to the father of Jayavarman VII, this late-12th century Buddhist shrine has several *gopuras* with four smiling faces on top. The eastern *gopura* is being split and crushed simultaneously by a ficus tree and makes for a great photo. Surrounded by three laterite walls, the temple is built on a single level and contains some fine carvings.

Preah Khan

Located on the Grand Circuit and left, much like Ta Prohm, largely unrestored, Preah Khan is a huge sprawling temple complex of rectangular enclosures around a typically small Buddhist sanctuary. Also like Ta Prohm, the temple was built during the reign of Jayavarman VII in the late 12th and early 13th centuries, and served as a center of learning and meditation. It also had an equally impressive retinue. More than 100,000 people were connected to Preah Khan, a royal city in its hey-day, supporting more than 1,000 teachers as well as 1,000 dancers.

Preah Khan means "sacred sword," a reference to a sacred sword that Jayavarman II, the first Angkorian king, handed to his successor—and which was subsequently handed down from generation to generation. The words "Preah Khan" are Siamese. though, so the story of the sword could have originated there.

Consecrated in 1191, Preah Khan stands on two older palace complexes. The process of anastylosis, the dismantling and rebuilding of a structure, has been utilized here. In the 1930s, the jungle (except for the large trees) was removed, making the site much more accessible. Nevertheless, the trees around the site remain impressive, and with fewer visitors than Ta Prohm, Preah Khan is a good place to witness the interplay between stone and nature in peace.

Preah Khan was a temple of the Mahayana Buddhist sect, and many of its carvings were disfigured and destroyed following the death of Jayavarman VII and Angkor's brief return to Hinduism. Within its enclosure, Preah Khan contains many smaller independent Hindu shrines and temples. The temple complex was built right to the shore of the Jayatataka Baray, to the east. It's best to enter from this side.

Preah Khan has four enclosure walls, the longest of which runs 700 by 800 meters. The complex was once surrounded by a moat and spreads across an area of some 140 hectares. This outer wall, constructed of laterite, contains sandstone sculptures of *garudas,* formerly topped by Buddhist images, long destroyed, at 50-meter intervals all the way around the complex. Four gates, at the cardinal points, offer access. Each entrance features a causeway crossing the moat, lined by gods and demons carrying *naga* snakes, similar to the causeways at the gates of Angkor Thom.

Visitors first come upon the Hall of Dancers. The lintels above the eight doorways all feature exquisite carvings of dancing *apsaras.* Just to the north of this building, a structure of unknown purpose has baffled scientists for decades: a two-story building with no discernable stairway and round columns, similar to Greek designs and unique to Angkor. The inner enclosures around the sanctuary can appear labyrinthine, due to the many galleries, low corridors, and walls with false windows. The walls used to be covered with huge bronze plates. The inner sanctuary today is a stone stupa, which was added many years after the temple's inception.

The Western Baray and Western Mebon

The Western Baray, located a few kilometers north of Siem Reap International Airport, is an incredible 8 kilometers by 2.3 kilometers wide, and continues to carry water year-round. On weekends, it's a favorite picnic spot. Snacks and drinks are sold at stalls along the dam on the southern side of the reservoir. In the center of the *baray,* the Western Mebon, a small temple in ruinous condition built in the 11th century during the reign of Udayadityavarman, can be visited by boat and features remarkable carvings of animals. The Western Baray is off the usual temple circuits, but it's worth a visit for its local life and the lack of crowds.

The Roluos Group

The Roluos Group of temples, named for its proximity to the modern village of Roluos, was part of the city of Hariharalaya, the first great Khmer capital. Located some 13 kilometers southeast of Siem Reap and founded by Jayavarman II in the early 9th century, Hariharalaya was the template for the later building frenzies of the Khmer kings. It was the first royal city established in the Angkor area and remained the capital of the Khmer for 70 years. Its last ruler, Yasovarman I, was the first king to build a temple at Angkor, at Phnom Bakheng, where he moved the capital in 905. The temples of this era were built of brick, and feature high and square towers on low bases. Structures such as *gopura* and libraries were first introduced during this time.

The detour to the Roluos temples is well worth the effort and entrance fees are covered by the pass to the Angkor Archaeological Park. There are three major temples at Roluos: Preah Ko, Bakong, and Lolei, all of them dedicated to Hindu deities.

Preah Ko was one of the very first temples built at Hariharalaya, and hence one of the first temples built in the Angkor area. Its outer walls have almost gone, so the temple complex seems quite small today, but it's well worth a visit, not least for its exquisite carvings. Preah Ko means "temple of the bull," named after stone *nandis* (sacred bulls), remnants of which stand on the eastern side of the temple. Originally, the building was surrounded by a moat and traversed by causeways. Beyond the *nandis,* a brick

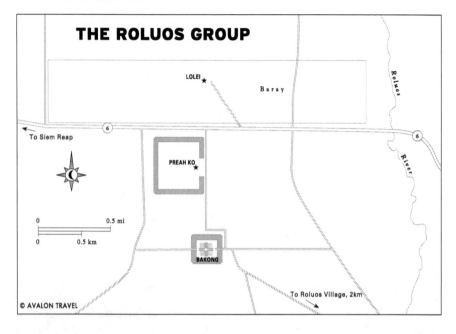

THE ROLUOS GROUP

LOLEI ★

Baray

To Siem Reap

PREAH KO ★

0   0.5 mi

0   0.5 km

BAKONG

To Roluos Village, 2km

© AVALON TRAVEL

Roluos

River

wall, pierced by two *gopuras* to the east and west, contains the sanctuary: a low platform with six brick towers. Unlike other temples, Preah Ko does not seem to be too concerned with symmetry. The six towers are not evenly spaced and those to the east are larger than the ones to the west. Preah Ko was dedicated to the king's ancestors and each tower contained a Hindu deity. The carved decorations on the towers' false doors, columns, and lintels are worth checking out. The three towers to the east feature male guardians and are thought to have been dedicated to paternal ancestors, while the towers to the west have female goddesses flanking the doorways and were most likely dedicated to maternal ancestors.

The **Bakong** was built after the death of Jayavarman II, and it became state temple of the Khmer Empire during the reign of Indravarman I. It stood at the heart of the city of Hariharalaya. The Bakong was the first temple-mountain built by a Khmer king and, dedicated to Shiva, its sanctuary probably contained a lingam. The site is surrounded

by a rectangular wall 900 meters by 700 meters long, which in turn was surrounded by a moat. Causeways lead through the outer wall, lined with *naga* balustrades. An inner wall can be passed through four *gopuras* located at the cardinal points. The temple faces east, so it's best to enter from that side. As at Preah Khan, there's a processional space, lined with stone serpents to pass before reaching the inner compound. Numerous well-preserved buildings stand to the left and right: libraries, *dharamshalas* (rest houses), and what are assumed to be crematoriums. Set around the platform that the sanctuary stands on are eight brick towers, open to the east only, their stairways guarded by stone lions. The towers have false doors in the other directions, featuring fine carvings. The platform the sanctuary sits on is built in five levels. On the first three levels, stone elephants—they get smaller as one ascends—stand on the corners. The fourth level is dominated by 12 sandstone towers, each of which contains a lingam. The sanctuary itself, a square tower with a lotus spire, was built later than the rest of the temple, probably in the 12th century.

The temple of **Lolei,** built a little later than the other two monuments at Roluos, was erected during the reign of Yasovarman I and was dedicated to Shiva. Originally Lolei stood on an island in the middle of a huge *baray,* which helped to irrigate the area around Hariharalaya and was the first reservoir built by a Khmer king. Lolei features just four brick towers, all of them in poor and overgrown condition, but some incredible carvings and inscriptions remain. An active modern pagoda operates within the temple compound.

Banteay Samre

Banteay Samre is a little bit out of the way and is best visited while on the way to or from Banteay Srei. It's worth the effort though, as the road to the temple leads through local villages and open countryside. The mid-12th century Hindu temple, built during the reign of Suryavarman II, is located on the eastern side of the Eastern Baray and resembles Angkor Wat in style, though not in dimensions. The temple's name refers to a group or tribe of people, possibly an indigenous minority related to the Khmer, who used to live around Phnom Kulen and is mentioned in an interesting folk story.

Banteay Samre has been reconstructed utilizing the anastylosis technique (the complete disassembling and rebuilding of a structure), and by all accounts was just a pile of rubble prior to the restoration works. The Banteay Samre complex is square in shape and features a moat, now dry, within its outermost enclosure wall, which in turn is pierced by four *gopuras* at the cardinal points. The wall around the inner temple complex is raised above floor level and features pavilions on its four corners. It's best to enter through the eastern *gopura* into the inner part of the temple. This route leads to a platform and a long hall that in turn leads to the central sanctuary. Two libraries can be seen to the north and south of the hall. Banteay Samre sees relatively few visitors. Curiously, the upper reliefs of the sanctuary feature Buddhist scenes.

THE STORY OF BANTEAY SAMRE

Once upon a time, a farmer named Pou, a member of the Samre community, an indigenous minority living near the Kulen mountain, got hold of seeds with supernatural powers. He planted the seeds and soon harvested the most delicious sweet cucumbers anyone had ever tasted. As a sign of respect, he took his harvest before the king, who found them so tasty that he ordered Pou to kill anyone who might enter his field. During the rainy season, the royal household ran out of cucumbers and the king himself decided to visit Pou for more. But the king arrived at Pou's field after dark and the farmer, thinking the monarch an intruder, killed him with a spear. Pou buried the king in the center of his field. As the king had no descendents, his advisors sought the wisdom of a Victory Elephant, as to who should be the successor. The elephant promptly marched to Pou's field and identified the farmer as the rightful ruler. Pou had himself crowned but the court dignitaries refused to show him respect; after all, he was just a Samre. Frustrated, Pou left the capital and moved to Banteay Samre. He called all the court's dignitaries, and all those who showed respect to the royal regalia of his predecessor were decapitated. Overcome by Pou's compassion, the remaining dignitaries accepted his authority and the kingdom has been ruled in harmony ever after.

◖ Banteay Srei

Banteay Srei, the "Citadel of Women," lies 38 kilometers (around 30–40 minutes in a tuk-tuk) from Siem Reap and is a little off the usual temple circuit. But this late-10th century temple complex, though modest in size, is one of the highlights of the Angkor Archaeological Park and should not be missed. It features some of the finest carvings in the world and has been extremely well restored.

Small by the usual bombastic dimensions of

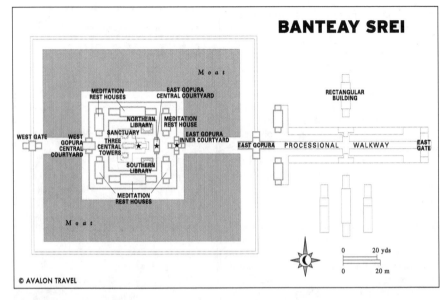

BANTEAY SREI

Moat

RECTANGULAR BUILDING

MEDITATION REST HOUSES

EAST GOPURA CENTRAL COURTYARD

NORTHERN LIBRARY

MEDITATION REST HOUSE

SANCTUARY

EAST GOPURA INNER COURTYARD

WEST GATE

WEST GOPURA CENTRAL COURTYARD

THREE CENTRAL TOWERS

EAST GOPURA   PROCESSIONAL   WALKWAY   EAST GATE

SOUTHERN LIBRARY

MEDITATION REST HOUSES

Moat

0   20 yds
0   20 m

© AVALON TRAVEL

Khmer monuments, Banteay Srei was built during the reign of Rajendravarman. It's the only temple known to have been built not under the authority of a king, but by Yajnyavaraha, a Brahmin advisor to the king, who dedicated the complex to Shiva. Originally the site was called Tribhuvanamahesvara, or Isvarapura. Banteay Srei was once enclosed by three walls and a moat, though only two walls remain today. Entrance is best through a *gopura* on the temple's east side. Before reaching the central temple compound, visitors pass along a processional walkway flanked by galleries, walls, and more *gopuras*. To the north of the walkway, a single building features a brilliant carving of Vishnu as man-lion. Step into the inner compound through another *gopura* and you are facing the central part with the best carvings. All around the compound, six annex buildings may have served as meditation rest houses. Inside the temple compound, virtually every bit of wall space is covered in exquisite carvings. The soft, red sandstone can be carved almost like wood and therefore allows for incredible detail and texture. The central shrines, three in all, were dedicated to Shiva

and Vishnu and are guarded by mythical figures with human bodies and animal heads. These are replicas: The originals have been stolen or removed for safekeeping. The walls are covered with carved foliage, as well as geometric patterns. The central towers are covered with male and female divinities. The females wear such heavy earrings that their ear lobes are elongated. The lintels above the doorways to the central sanctuary are embellished with scenes from the *Ramayana,* including the abduction of Sita.

Two libraries to the east of the central sanctuary, made of brick, laterite, and sandstone, also feature outstanding carvings. The eastern side of the northern library (on the right as you approach from the east) is decorated by depictions of Indra, god of the sky, as he scatters celestial rain across the building's eastern side, while a *naga* snake rises from the deluge. The western side depicts Krishna killing his cruel uncle, King Kamsa, as shocked women look on.

The southern library's western side is covered in carvings telling the story of Parvati trying to attract Shiva, who is in deep meditation.

Parvati gets Kama, god of love, to shoot an arrow into Shiva's heart. Shiva promptly gets angry and burns Kama to ashes. He does notice Parvati, however, marries her, and brings Kama back to life. If only things were as simple in real life...

On the eastern side of the southern library, a scene from the *Ramayana* unfolds. Ravana, king of the demons of Lanka, tries to gain access to Mount Kailash, home of Shiva and Parvati. As he is barred from entering, he lifts the entire mountain and shakes it. Shiva in turn brings down the mountain on top of Ravana, who acknowledges Shiva's might and sings his name in praise for a thousand years.

Banteay Srei was further expanded in the 11th century and was probably in use until the 14th century. Yet the temple complex was not "discovered" by the French until 1914 and became famous only when celebrated French writer André Malraux tried to steal four *devatas* (goddesses) in 1923. During the 1930s, Banteay Srei was the first Angkor monument to benefit from the process of anastylosis, and it was only in 1936 that the true age of the temple was established. Sadly, the temple has been looted several times since Malraux's early efforts to deplete Cambodia's heritage and even concrete replicas of sculptures that have been moved to Angkor Conservation have been attacked.

Banteay Srei is best seen in the early morning or late afternoon, when the red sandstone really comes to life. Because of its modest size, the site tends to be overcrowded, but by late afternoon (the temple closes at 5 P.M.), the big groups have left.

Kbal Spean

Some 12 kilometers beyond Banteay Srei, the riverbed of Kbal Spean makes for an interesting detour during and after the rainy season. This "River of a Thousand Lingas" lies at the foot of Phnom Kulen and features impressive carvings of lingas and several figures in its rocky riverbed. To get to the river section with the carvings, it's a 40-minute walk. Note that this site closes at 3 P.M., so it's probably

PHALLIC OR NOT? – THE CULT OF THE LINGA

The linga, or lingam, according to Merriam-Webster's dictionary is "a stylized phallic symbol that is worshipped in Hinduism as a sign of generative power that represents the god Shiva." In fact, there is no agreement amongst scholars, mystics, and academics what the linga actually represents. It's thought that perhaps the linga was initially understood simply as a cylindrical shape which represented the formlessness of creation, and later became associated with Shiva. Later still, the linga came to be seen as the divine phallus of Shiva and was worshipped as a representation of the creator and destroyer of the universe.

Usually the linga rests on a square pedestal, called *uma*, or yoni, which is widely believed to represent the vagina. Some scholars and mystics such as Swami Vivekananda and Christopher Isherwood disagree with this latter interpretation.

Everyone agrees, though, that the linga has been worshipped for a very long time. It precedes Hinduism and has its origins either in early Buddhism or animism. It goes back at least to the Indus Valley civilization. In Cambodia, linga are found everywhere around Angkor and pre-Angkorian temple sites, perhaps first introduced by Jayavarman II. Linga are usually in temple sanctuaries, where worshippers have been pouring water over them for centuries. As a result, the water is said to become sacred. One of the most spectacular linga sites around Angkor is Kbal Spean, where hundreds of linga have been carved into the rocky riverbed. The water rushes across the carved stones and then feeds the rice fields below, perhaps symbolizing fertility. It's best to visit in the rainy season, or just after, when the river carries enough water to give the site some ambience.

best visited in the morning or around noon (as you'll be walking through forest, it shouldn't be too hot). The area around the carvings can be quite polluted by plastic, left by picnickers. Even here, some carvings have been hacked out of the river by looters in recent years. There's also a waterfall, with some carvings on top. Do not stroll off the well-trodden paths into the forest as the area may still be mined.

VICINITY OF ANGKOR
◖ Beng Melea

No doubt one of the most stunning temples in Cambodia, Beng Melea is still somewhat off the beaten track, but this atmospheric jungle ruin is bound to see a lot more visitors in the near future as roads improve. Built in the early 11th century during the reign of Suryavarman II, this temple compound is about one square kilometer in size, roughly precedes the design of Angkor Wat (though there are no bas-reliefs here), and stands on an ancient Khmer crossroad between Angkor, Koh Ker, and Preah Vihear.

More than any temple in the Angkor Archaeological Park, Beng Melea is an experience. Overgrown by jungle and collapsed on itself, the compound is a huge jumble of broken towers, underground galleries, and unidentifiable piles of rubble, massive walls, and corridors, adorned with false doors and windows and split open by roots that have been pushing apart the brickwork for centuries. Temples don't come any more Lost World than this.

Have a local guide show you incredible corners and pathways where the first rays of the sun break in long thin strips of bright light through the tall trees that grow out of the temple walls and play over the smiling faces of *apsaras,* the temple's celestial dancers. To make access a little easier, a wooden walkway was constructed during the shooting of the French movie *Two Brothers* by Jean-Jacques Annaud in 2002, a tale of two tiger cubs in colonial Cambodia.

The main temple itself is surrounded by a moat and several outbuildings, possibly libraries and *dharamshalas* (royal guesthouses), and is reached via a broad causeway lined with *naga* snakes. Until recently, Beng Melea was heavily

the central courtyard of Beng Melea at sunrise

© TOM VATER

BEYOND THE TOURIST TRAIL: CAMBODIA'S BEST REMOTE TEMPLE SITES

While the temples around Siem Reap now see literally millions of visitors, it requires only a little extra effort to escape the crowds and check out some more remote locations where you might find yourself almost alone amongst splendid Khmer ruins. And if you're interested in a trip deep into the Cambodian jungles, more gigantic temple complexes await you. Don't stray off the beaten tracks, though, as some remote temples could still be mined.

Here is a list of the country's best remote temple sites, in order of preference:

- **Beng Melea** – Spectacular 12th-century jungle temple, 70 kilometers northeast of Siem Reap, far enough away to avoid the crowds. Large parts of this huge compound have collapsed, and high walls, underground passages, and huge creeper trees make for an eerie atmosphere.

- **Koh Ker** – Almost an archaeological park in its own right, the 10th-century Koh Ker complex, a former Khmer capital 70 kilometers northeast of Siem Reap, contains almost a hundred monuments, including the impressive Prasat Thom, a seven-tiered pyramid in a jungle clearing. The area is still being de-mined, and despite good road connections, relatively few visitors make it out here.

- **Banteay Chhmar** – An overgrown, remote, 12th-century temple site featuring towers with the faces carrying the *sourir Khmer*, the famous Khmer smile. Despite heavy looting in recent times, this temple site, 61 kilometers north of Sisophon, is worth visiting for its ruined grandeur and sheer remoteness.

- **Preah Vihear** – Breathtaking views reward arduous travelers who brave dust and potholes to reach this cliff-top border temple, in recent times the center of political and military tensions between Cambodia and Thailand.

- **Preah Khan** – Truly a lost site in Preah Vihear Province, the roads to this remote temple complex north of Kompong Thom are so bad that the site is only accessible by motorbike – or, if you have the funds, by helicopter from Siem Reap. A road will no doubt be built soon, but for the moment, Preah Khan remains the most remote temple complex in Cambodia.

- **Wat Athvea** – A small Angkor-era temple in good condition, located just six kilometers south of Siem Reap on the road to the Tonlé Sap Lake, is flanked by an active pagoda and a friendly village. It's not truly remote, but it's rarely visited.

mined. On my first visit in 2001, warning signs still surrounded the entire compound and de-mining continued into 2007. Stick to the well-trodden paths.

In front of the temple, several small restaurants, which serve cheap Cambodian standards and cold drinks, are lined up by the roadside. Entrance to the temple is US$5 and tickets must be purchased from the guards on the causeway approaching the main (thoroughly collapsed) gate. The ticket for the Angkor Archaeological Park is not valid to visit this temple.

Beng Melea lies some 70 kilometers to the northeast of Siem Reap and can easily be reached on a one-day round-trip in a car or on a motorbike. Follow Route 6 from Siem Reap towards Phnom Penh and turn left at the small town of Dam Dek. From here it's another 35 kilometers. Alternatively, head for Banteay Srei and then Phnom Kulen and follow the base of the mountain for 25 kilometers until you reach a crossing where you turn left onto a mostly tarmac road, which takes you to the temple after another 10 kilometers. Note that this road is private; bikes have to pay US$1 while taxis are charged US$2.50, each way. Unfortunately, there are no accommodations around the temple yet. A taxi from Siem Reap should cost around US$60, and a *motodup* at least US$25.

Phnom Krom

For great views over the Tonlé Sap Lake, head for Phnom Krom mountain, some 10 kilometers to the south of Siem Reap on the shores of the lake. On top of the hill, an active pagoda is popular with locals and there are also a number of towers from the 11th century. Since 2006, Phnom Krom has been considered part of the Angkor Archaeological Park and can only be visited with a valid ticket. Though there's no ticket booth here, guards sometimes demand to see a pass, and as this minor ruin is far removed from other temples, very few people make it up here nowadays.

A tuk-tuk to Phnom Krom and back will cost you around US$5.

Chong Khneas Floating Village

Chong Khneas, populated largely by Vietnamese, is the floating village on the Tonlé Sap Lake closest to Siem Reap, and has seen a great deal of tourist traffic in recent years. As with other floating villages, expect to see schools, clinics, gas stations, and family homes, as well as souvenir shops. You will also see lots of boats filled with tour groups here. An interesting stopover in the village is the **Gecko Environment Center** (http://jinja.apsara.org/gecko/gecko.htm), which informs visitors about the unique biodiversity of the area. If you have time and want to see more of traditional life on the Tonlé Sap, skip Chong Khneas and visit Kompong Luong near Pursat or the floating community near Kompong Chhnang.

There are several possibilities to get out to see this waterborne community. The cheapest way might be to go directly to the boat dock and get on one of the many tour boats waiting. Two-hour trips should be about US$10, though you'll share the ride with a big group. More laid-back and intimate experiences are offered by **H2O** (tel. 012/809010), which operates a smart little aluminum boat that seats just eight passengers and offers cruises with drinks. Alternatively, the most stylish way to get on the water is with the **Tara River Boat** (tel. 092/957765, www.taraboat.com), a larger wooden vessel that offers a number of different trips on the lake. A half-day outing (four hours) is US$20 a person, and includes transportation from and to your hotel, a light meal, and drinks. Tours run at 7 A.M., 9 A.M., and 11 A.M. This trip also runs by a crocodile farm. A sunset trip, with dinner and unlimited drinks, costs US$30 and departs at 3:30 P.M.

To get there by yourself, take the road from Siem Reap to Phnom Krom, towards the lake. As you approach the lake, you'll reach the departure point for the ferries to Phnom Penh and Battambang. A tuk-tuk should be US$6 for the round-trip. Many tuk-tuk drivers get commission from agents offering boat tours. If you refuse to go with the outfit suggested by your driver, you may cause offense.

Prek Toal Bird Sanctuary

The biosphere and bird sanctuary Prek Toal is almost as over-run by commerce as Chong Khneas. It takes about two hours to get there in a boat, and you should expect to slide through tall grasses and brackish water. If you come in the dry season, you might be able to spot storks, ibis, pelicans, and eagles.

If you organize everything yourself, a boat to the Prek Toal Research Station will cost around US$50, where visitors have to pay an entrance fee of US$5—as well as another US$25 for a guided boat tour of the sanctuary itself. Many guesthouses and tour operators arrange packages at similar or just slightly higher prices. Try Peace of Angkor Tours (www.peaceofangkor.com). **Tara River Boat** (tel. 092/957765, www.taraboat.com) offers a day trip with transfers, all fees, drinks, and an English-speaking guide for US$60 per person.

Serious bird-watchers might want to check the website of the **Sam Veasna Center** (tel. 063/761597, www.samveasna.org), which specializes in bird-watching expeditions to remote sights.

To reach Prek Toal, use the same route as to Chong Khneas.

Kompong Phluk

This group of three traditional Khmer villages rises out of the Tonlé Sap floodplain on high stilts. About 3,000 people live here during the wet season among mangrove forests. In the dry season, when the lake's waters recede and leave the houses like stranded storks on their six-meter-high poles, many inhabitants move into smaller huts on stilts farther into the lake. The people of Kompong Phluk live off fishing and shrimp harvesting.

There are two ways to get to Kompong Phluk. In the rainy season, take a boat from Chong Khneas (US$50 for two passengers for a half-day excursion). In the dry season, when water levels are low, it's possible to drive all the way to the community, some 16 kilometers south of Siem Reap. Alternatively, depending on water levels, you might be able to get a boat from the village near the Roluos Group of temples.

Kompong Kleang

With more than 10,000 inhabitants, Kompong Kleang is the largest community on the lake. Most of the community, about 35 kilometers north of Siem Reap, is built on wooden poles anchored in the lakebed. The people here are Khmer and live off fishing. So far, visitor numbers are far fewer than at Chong Khneas, but more and more tour operators are putting this unique community on their itineraries. Around the village, flooded forest provides important spawning grounds for the Tonlé Sap's fish population. In the wet season, the houses are a couple of meters above the waterline, but once the waters have receded, the stilts can reach 10 meters above the muddy soil—quite a sight.

To get to Kompong Kleang, depending on the season and prevailing water levels, you might be able to head for Chong Khneas and catch a boat from there, or head east on Route 6 to Domdek Village, from where it's a short boat ride (US$10) in the wet season, or a longer bike ride all the way to Kompong Kleang in the dry season.

Phnom Kulen

Phnom Kulen is a mountain and something of a private national park. Inside the park, a waterfall is quite impressive in the rainy season. A River of a Thousand Lingas, on the other hand, is best seen in the dry season, when stone carvings (similar to those at Kbal Spean, a site that is included in the Angkor Pass) in the riverbed are clearly visible. Cambodians consider Phnom Kulen the cradle of the Khmer Empire—it was here that Jayavarman II declared a unified nation under a single ruler in A.D. 802. Hence the spot gets very crowded with picnickers on weekends and there can be quite a lot of garbage lying around.

What's more, entry to the site is US$20. (Entry to national parks in Cambodia is usually US$5, but Phnom Kulen is under the authority of a Cambodian businessman with good political connections.) The fee is as much as a day around Angkor Wat, even before your transportation costs are factored in; considering that there are no remarkable ruins to see here, for many it's not worth it—unless you're a waterfall fanatic.

It's possible to hire a *motodup* for the hundred-kilometer round-trip for around US$15, or a taxi for around US$30. From the ticket booth of the park entrance, it's 10 kilometers to the waterfall. If you are prepared to walk from here, the entrance fee is reduced to US$10.

www.moon.com

MOON.COM is ready to help plan your next trip! Filled with fresh trip ideas and strategies, author interviews, informative travel blogs, a detailed map library, and descriptions of all the Moon guidebooks, Moon.com is all you need to get out and explore the world—or even places in your own backyard. While at Moon.com, sign up for our monthly e-newsletter for updates on new releases, travel tips, and expert advice from our on-the-go Moon authors. As always, when you travel with Moon, expect an experience that is uncommon and truly unique.

MOON IS ON FACEBOOK—BECOME A FAN!
JOIN THE MOON PHOTO GROUP ON FLICKR

MAP SYMBOLS

▨▨▨	Expressway	**(**	Highlight	✗	Airfield	⚲	Golf Course
▨▨▨	Primary Road	○	City/Town	✈	Airport	**P**	Parking Area
▨▨▨	Secondary Road	◉	State Capital	▲	Mountain	⬭	Archaeological Site
▨▨▨	Unpaved Road	⊛	National Capital	✛	Unique Natural Feature	⚑	Church
- - - - -	Trail	★	Point of Interest			⛽	Gas Station
•••••••	Ferry	•	Accommodation	🌫	Waterfall	⬭	Glacier
⤬⤬⤬	Railroad	▼	Restaurant/Bar	♠	Park	⬭	Mangrove
▨▨▨	Pedestrian Walkway	■	Other Location	**T**	Trailhead	⬭	Reef
▨▨▨	Stairs	⋀	Campground	⛷	Skiing Area	⬭	Swamp

CONVERSION TABLES

°C = (°F - 32) / 1.8
°F = (°C x 1.8) + 32
1 inch = 2.54 centimeters (cm)
1 foot = 0.304 meters (m)
1 yard = 0.914 meters
1 mile = 1.6093 kilometers (km)
1 km = 0.6214 miles
1 fathom = 1.8288 m
1 chain = 20.1168 m
1 furlong = 201.168 m
1 acre = 0.4047 hectares
1 sq km = 100 hectares
1 sq mile = 2.59 square km
1 ounce = 28.35 grams
1 pound = 0.4536 kilograms
1 short ton = 0.90718 metric ton
1 short ton = 2,000 pounds
1 long ton = 1.016 metric tons
1 long ton = 2,240 pounds
1 metric ton = 1,000 kilograms
1 quart = 0.94635 liters
1 US gallon = 3.7854 liters
1 Imperial gallon = 4.5459 liters
1 nautical mile = 1.852 km

°FAHRENHEIT · °CELSIUS

°FAHRENHEIT	°CELSIUS	
230	110	
220	100	WATER BOILS
210		
200	90	
190	80	
180		
170	70	
160		
150	60	
140	50	
130		
120		
110	40	
100	30	
90		
80	20	
70		
60	10	
50		
40	0	WATER FREEZES
30		
20	-10	
10		
0	-20	
-10		
-20	-30	
-30		
-40	-40	

INCH 0 1 2 3 4

CM 0 1 2 3 4 5 6 7 8 9 10

MOON ANGKOR WAT
Avalon Travel
a member of the Perseus Books Group
1700 Fourth Street
Berkeley, CA 94710, USA
www.moon.com

Editor and Series Manager: Kathryn Ettinger
Copy Editor: Ellie Behrstock
Graphics Coordinators: Domini Dragoone, Amber
  Pirker
Production Coordinator: Domini Dragoone
Cover Designer: Domini Dragoone
Map Editor: Brice Ticen
Cartographer: Kat Bennett
Proofreader: Margo Winton

ISBN: 978-1-59880-561-1

Front cover photo: Buddha with orange shroud at
  Angkor Wat © Michael James | Dreamstime.com
Title page photo: Tree root at Angkor Wat ©
  123rf.com/SueiKae Wong

Printed in the United States

ABOUT THE AUTHOR

Tom Vater

Tom Vater first visited Cambodia in 2001 to document the indigenous minorities in Mondulkiri for the British Library's International Sound Archive, and instantly fell in love with the country. A year later, Tom cowrote and production-managed a documentary on Angkor for German-French television, which gave him the opportunity to spend several weeks among the country's temples. Since then, he has returned to Cambodia several times each year to cover its politics and culture for various publications. On his journeys around the country, he has encountered kings, pilgrims, soldiers, secret agents, pirates, hippies, policemen, and prophets. Every one of them put up with him for longer than he deserved.

Tom has been writing and traveling in Southeast Asia since 1993. He is the author of numerous books and has cowritten several documentary screenplays for European television. He is a regular contributor to the South Eastern Globe, one of Cambodia's English-language magazines. His feature articles, mostly on Asian subjects and destinations, have appeared around the world in publications such as *The Asia Wall Street Journal, The South China Morning Post, The Far Eastern Economic Review,* **and** *Marie Claire.*

Tom often works with his wife, photographer Aroon Thaewchatturat, with whom he shares a home in Bangkok and has published three photo books on South Asia. Visit his website at www.tomvater.com.